"*Becoming Free* is a book that changed the way I view life. I'm more present and able to enjoy every moment on a deeper level."

~ Ebony Anderberg, twin mom, fitness entrepreneur, and model

"This book is for those who seem to get tangled in a web of wisdom and wonder how to decipher what's true for themselves. Amanda's story invites you on a journey with so many twists and turns, thumps and bumps that it takes a bit to realize that the author is simply taking you on a tour of her actual magnificent heart."

~ Rita Kampen, author of *Smash*

"Becoming Free is a powerful exploration of breaking free from all expectations and embarking on the path to authentic living, leaving the reader feeling liberated and empowered to embrace their true selves. This book takes the reader on a transformative journey of acceptance, empowering each of us to wholeheartedly embrace all facets of our existence."

~ Gabriella Cacciatore, author and coach

"*Becoming Free* is a book about the curious, adamant, and powerful human spirit that never stops believing, searching for meaning, and discovering, despite all the obstacles and unwanted outcomes. Amanda brought me to a world full of magic amidst the pain, full of hope amidst the hopelessness, full of strength amidst the weakness, full of God's love amidst the loneliness. I was astonished to see how all the versions of the self ultimately transformed the never-ending longing into peace, happiness, and safety that are simply a projection of inner satisfaction, not connected to anything that we, as a society, consider as a 'success.' Isn't that the ultimate desire for all of us?!"

~ Diyana Dimitrova, cognitive hypnotherapist, author, and podcast host

"*Becoming Free* is an inspiring book for all seekers, adventurers, and lovers of life. Follow Amanda on her own journey to explore non-attachment, release fear, and step into greater freedom. In doing so, you might just gain your own. Fresh perspectives and new possibilities await you on every page. Dive in and enjoy the journey!"

~ Jaime Fleres, author of *Birth Your Story* and founder of Whale Song

"This book takes the reader on a journey of self-inquiry, empowering each of us to remember that liberation always starts and ends with self-acceptance and love! Amanda's courage to expose her journey and process is so inspiring. Every person on a spiritual journey can take so much away from this raw, authentic, and honest memoir."

~ Cara Busacker, energetic movement guide and healer

"*Becoming Free* is a captivating memoir that delves deep into the universal quest for inner peace and freedom. Through Amanda's remarkable journey, readers are invited to explore the raw and unfiltered experience of embracing vulnerability and diving headfirst into life's constant challenges. Amanda fearlessly confronts her own vulnerabilities, offering a poignant portrayal of the human experience in its entirety. Her courage serves as a beacon of inspiration, illuminating the path toward personal liberation and authenticity. This book reminds us all of the transformative power of embracing our true selves. A must-read for anyone seeking to cultivate bravery, resilience, and a deeper connection to the essence of life."

~ Tara Davis, channel for the Beings of Light and author of *Becoming Tara*

"*Becoming Free* embarks on a profound exploration of the intricate dance between non-attachment, resistance, and acceptance, offering readers a transformative journey toward inner peace and freedom. Amanda's candid narrative delves into her personal odyssey, unraveling the layers of self-awareness and self-discovery with raw vulnerability and profound insight. Experience an internal shift as you explore your own relationship with acceptance by opening your awareness to embrace the present moment in its entirety, free from judgment or resistance. If you're looking for inner liberation, this is a must-read!"

~ Lynn Morgan Carpenter, intuitive medium, life coach, and transformational speaker

"*Becoming Free* is an intimate journey through the complex tapestry of human emotion, desire, and the pursuit of freedom. Amanda masterfully conveys a narrative that is as much about surrendering to life's unpredictability as it is about the active pursuit of personal dreams.

It is a heart-wrenching portrayal of the protagonist's internal battle with the reality of unfulfilled expectations. Amanda's candid writing style lays bare the soul's deepest yearnings and disappointments, resonating deeply with anyone who's ever grappled with the dissonance between life's harsh realities and the fervent desires of the heart. Her stories in romantic Italy, beautiful Costa Rica, and sunny Florida, contrasting with the darkness of her inner turmoil, is a poignant reminder of the often invisible struggles we all face.

Amanda delves into the liberation that comes from letting go of the incessant need to control life's outcomes. Her exploration of faith and intuition is a refreshing take on the often-overlooked aspect of personal growth. This serves as a gentle nudge towards embracing life's spontaneous nature and finding freedom in the unpredictable."

~ Clinton Brown, entrepreneur, community builder, and inseminator of ideas

"Amanda has a way of coming out of the pages you're reading and embracing you in a warm hug that makes you feel like everything is going to be okay and that you are loved. This story is a must-read for all of those who are 'sick of getting in their own way' and ready to move beyond the constant self-reflection and into the action of living a free and abundant life. In a world where self-development and becoming conscious are at our fingertips, where do we draw the line when it comes to 'doing the work' and living our lives? Amanda has the wisdom and ability to share with us how to let it all go and feel safe and supported in a way we never have before in doing so. A beautiful book."

~ Emily East, speaker and author of *Like a Mother*

"This book will bring the reader a sense of possibility and peace. In a society that offers many recipes for happiness that depend on certain criteria, I found Amanda's words brought a new perspective. She reminded me that as I accept every moment exactly as it is and begin to live my life without resistance or judgment to what is, I am able to experience each moment to its fullest. When I am willing to feel everything, I free myself and everyone around me. I encourage each reader to view Amanda's story as an example for any of us to become free."

~ Marjorie Warkentin, life path mentor and author of *Saying Yes to Life*

"*Becoming Free* is a soulful and honest reminder that, no matter what's happening to us, we are ultimately here to accept, to receive, and to love. Amanda shares her naked heart for you in these pages. It will melt yours if you let it."

~ David Sauvage, teacher of emotional intelligence
and founder of Culture of Healing

"Through the narration of Amanda's life, *Becoming Free* provides beautiful insight into a journey of self-inquiry and inner peace. With grace and authenticity, she shares her transformative journey, offering readers a roadmap to reclaim their own narrative and embrace the freedom that lies within. This book takes you on an intimate, personal journey of what it means to navigate the human experience."

~ Nikki Heyder, psychotherapist and yoga teacher

BECOMING FREE

BECOMING FREE

FROM LETTING GO
TO EMBRACING IT ALL

AMANDA JOHNSON

AWAKEN VILLAGE

PRESS

This is a work of nonfiction. Any resemblance to persons, living or dead, should be plainly apparent to them and those who know them, especially if the author has been kind enough to have provided their real names. All events described herein are from the author's perspective, with some of the details adjusted to protect confidentiality, some lost over time, and some recrafted to consolidate events and timelines.

The content of this book is for general instruction only. Each person's physical, emotional, and spiritual condition is unique. The instruction in this book is not intended to replace or interrupt the reader's relationship with a counselor, physician, or other mental health professional.

Editing by Grace Watson
Cover and interior design by Andrea Gibb
Author photo by Brian P. Wcislo

ISBN 978-1-957408-14-9 (paperback)
ISBN 978-1-957408-15-6 (ebook)

Library of Congress Control Number: 2023919837

Published by Awaken Village Press, Sioux Falls, SD
www.awakenvillagepress.com

For all those who forget they're already free.

"To detach is to move in time with life, to be in perfect accord with its changing music, and this is called Enlightenment."

- ALAN WATTS

CONTENTS

PART 3: NON-CHOOSING

PREFACE

If I were to tell you the only thing standing between you and true freedom is a matter of acceptance, what would you say? This is the question my soul asked me back in 2018 after I dove into being the non-judgmental observer and wrote my first book, *Becoming Enough*. That book took me and its readers on a journey to freeing oneself from the paralysis of perfectionism (or the misunderstandings of perfectionism), debilitating doubt, and constantly comparing oneself with others.

Alan Watts talks a lot about how the great fall of man occurred when we became self-aware. I was nearly complete with this book, *Becoming Free,* when I considered tossing the whole thing out because my writing of this book was amplifying and accentuating my already extreme self-awareness, and I no longer wanted to participate in the "getting in my own way" by spending more time contemplating and examining my life.

But I paused and breathed and decided that much like when I wrote and published my first book, the releasing of the book is the releasing of the very thing I'm writing about. Therefore, by writing and publishing this second book, I am letting go of my attachment to being overly self-aware, as in constantly analyzing and judging my actions and choices (not simply observing them) in the hope of understanding and knowing and feeling certain about things. I mean, there's no getting out of being self-aware. That's what being human is all about. But I am ready to free myself from the incessant nature of it. I am ready to accept that which I am aware of. I am ready to release my grip just a bit more. Yet I had to go into my self-awareness more to see just how self-aware I am. I had to go into the pain to find relief. Ironically, the very thing entrapping me is also the very thing that can free me.

Over the last decade, I've had numerous experiences that have liberated me little by little. I freed myself of anything that felt like it was constricting or limiting me. This started with the physical world—a husband, a career, an apartment, boxes of stuff. More recently (and perhaps most importantly), this transferred to my beliefs and emotional blocks.

I started to free myself from mental constructs—what I believed to be true, what I was telling myself, what I made things mean. Each of my beliefs, I questioned. I asked, "What if that isn't true?" I untangled all my old stories until I was left with very few. And I even noticed how the stories themselves played a part in my liberation. I had to create something from which to free myself. I believe we all do this. For some of us, we build homes and wealth and titles from which to free ourselves and learn to let go. For me, I built mental constructs from which I needed freeing. Though I imagine I'm not alone here and propose this is a major source of entrapment for most people too.

What I learned is that for everything I "lost," I got closer to the core of who I am. I went from freeing myself from as much as I could think of to accepting what is and claiming more and more of what I desired in my life. I eventually realized that by letting go, I am able to embrace more of what this life is all about.

I wrote this book because I am ready to truly become free. I am ready to embody what I have learned over the past many years about what true freedom means and watch it unfold in my life in magical, meaningful ways. I am ready to release any old stories or patterns I have when it comes to being attached to who I think I am, what I think I need to be okay, and any fears or doubts or insecurities and to finally step into who I truly am.

This book is my relief. And may it serve as yours too. May it high-light or point out the extreme to which we get in our own ways and keep ourselves stuck by thinking and over-analyzing and resisting and believing we're in control. May it release you to eventually understand that there is no right or wrong, good or bad, and invite you into the freedom of what the Taoists call "non-choosing." May it release you to be even more of who you are in each and every moment.

INTRODUCTION

People often say, "Freedom is the opportunity to choose." I used to believe this, until I further explored what choosing looks and feels like. When we are faced with choices, we might feel trapped or overwhelmed by needing to make the "right" or "best" choice. This is not freedom.

Some might say (and I, at times, agree) that we can choose how we feel and how we experience this world. This is where freedom and choosing go hand-in-hand. But there are layers of what we make choosing mean that we must move through first. And that is what this book is about. We first must remember that we always have a choice (and, in some ways, are always choosing). Then, we are invited to remember that there is no better or worse one. This is the tricky part yet where the greatest freedom is found.

When we practice the art of non-choosing, we are essentially accepting every single moment exactly as it is, acting or behaving or responding in whatever way we do and letting go of any attachment to the outcome, initiating the cycle all over again. There is no pushing or pulling. There is no longer a belief that the way we respond should be different or that our choices are not okay or that it will turn out a certain way.

This journey requires radical self-acceptance—letting go of any resistance to who we are or think we are. It asks that we simultaneously let go of attachment to thoughts and beliefs while radically accepting all of them. How do we do that?

For many of us, our beliefs and thoughts make up who we think we are. It can be very scary and destabilizing to question and let go of everything that makes you who you think you are. Yet this is where ultimate freedom is found. At least, I think. I can't say for sure, as I haven't arrived there yet (and maybe never will), but I can say that in the moments when I feel stuck or trapped, it's because I'm stuck or trapped in a belief or thought pattern. And when I can loosen my grip on it and either let it be or watch it go, I feel lighter and freer.

I set out to write a book on non-attachment, and when I started, I believed non-attachment looked a certain way. I thought it meant I couldn't have or want things—that if I did, I was attached to them. And if I was attached, then I would eventually get hurt. This showed up when it came to people, places, pets, and things. I was so afraid of being attached that I became attached to non-attachment.

This is why I had to take a long, hard look at my beliefs and see where I was still operating from fear or telling myself lies. I spent the past decade or more trying to convince myself that I didn't want or need certain things because I was so afraid of ultimately losing them. I figured if I wasn't attached to anything, I couldn't get hurt. But what I was actually attached to was my need to understand in order to protect myself from feeling pain.

Non-attachment isn't about avoiding pain; it's about letting all of it be, pain included. What I've learned on this journey to becoming free is that the more I am willing to feel, the more I am willing to have and want and be. And I don't need to be attached to any of it. Wanting something is natural, needing something is natural, having things is natural. Attachment happens when we get stuck, and this was often happening inside my head.

As I started to understand and practice the art of non-choosing, or as the Japanese say, "mushin" (no mind), I let every choice, action, thought, feeling, or outcome *be*. I started to practice what it feels like to "not mind" what happens. This is freedom.

Ultimately, the path to freedom is found when we free ourselves from the concepts of what any of this means and begin to live life without judgment or resistance to what is. When we experience each and every moment to its fullest, no longer afraid of "what might happen if …" or "what will they think …" or taking it personally or trying to control this thing called life, we are in a state of non-attachment. We don't mind what happens.

We don't get to force or manipulate our lives into being free—if I just do this or if they just do that, *then* I'll be free. And it doesn't look a certain way, such as freedom is having no responsibilities and traveling around the world or freedom is having a certain amount of money in the bank. This is why our external world does not need to change in order for us to feel (and be) free. We think letting go requires leaving or saying goodbye or throwing something away. But what if we stop pushing things away or pulling things toward us and instead let them be? Let our emotions be, let our actions be, let the outcomes be, let ourselves be?

When we do this, we expand our ability to be with what is, no matter what. Imagine our physical existence is a prison (I mean, most of us believe we are imprisoned one way or another already). The walls of the prison represent what we are willing to feel or tolerate in these physical, finite human bodies. And we can choose to either accept that we have physical bodies with physical experiences or fight against them or pretend they don't exist. And the more we accept the physical "limitations" by being willing to feel and experience everything, the more we create space and freedom to be exactly who we are meant to be in each and every moment.

Be prepared. The journey toward liberation is not an easy or comfortable one. It's sad and lonely at times. And the main reason is that it's entirely up to you. It's a journey of radical self-responsibility and self-acceptance. You do not get to point your finger at him or her or them and expect something different "out there" that will set you free. It's not the government or your boss or your partner or your kids that are keeping you trapped, imprisoning you. They are only able to do this to the degree you are already doing it to yourself. And you can't even point to other parts of you and say, "If only I were more ..." or "If only I could be less ...." That in and of itself is another trap. But as you begin to realize there is ultimately nothing to choose because you are willing to feel everything, you free yourself and everyone around you.

PART 1

NOT CHOOSING

CHAPTER 1

SAYING YES

As I stand in the doorway of my empty 1920s studio apartment, it looks so bare, so bright, the acoustics heightened as sounds bounce off the hardwood floors without the furniture to soak them up. These 450 square feet have served as my home for the past four years and have seen me through many transitions. It's the longest I have spent in any one place in more than thirteen years. With gratitude and trepidation, I place the key on a ledge by the doorway and, after looking back one last time, close the door behind me, feeling simultaneously confident and uncertain about my decision and what lies ahead.

Here I am at the age of thirty-three, leaving this city I have grown to love so much that my identity has wrapped itself up in. San Francisco—where I moved from Oakland after my divorce nearly ten years ago. Arriving here was a statement of breaking free and choosing what I wanted for one of the first times in my life. Another partnership later, I moved into this quaint studio on my own at the age of thirty. It has offered me a safe haven when, for the first time in my adult life, I became a single woman, gave online dating a brief go, traveled around the world before changing careers, and eventually started dating and then living with someone new. It was here I found myself letting go of who I thought I was, following my inner guidance and pursuing my passions, building a business (or at least attempting to), doing Bikram yoga, and getting to know myself better. And now, a bit older and wiser, I am taking life into my own hands (once again) and not yet sure what to do with it.

When I was twenty-seven, after nearly five years of being a working actor in one of the most expensive cities in the country, I walked away from my life as I knew it. Literally, in fact—over 2,000 miles along the Appalachian Trail, with no Plan B and no idea what would come next. This was a life-long dream for my then-boyfriend, Daniel, and I was happy to say yes (even if I had never spent a night in a tent or hiked more than a few miles). For nearly six months, I followed "Mr. Right" (the trail name he was immediately given) every step of the way.

Embarking on this dream of his also meant eventually giving up one of my own. Leaving theater wasn't an easy decision. Ever since I was a little girl, I had dreamed of being a famous actor. I got a degree in theater (nothing else, because my advisor told me that having a Plan B meant falling back on it—and I was going to become an actor, goshdarnit!), but it hadn't panned out the way I had thought it would. I was over it. I was done working my ass off. I was done "reaching and changing lives through the performing arts," as my longstanding resume claimed. I was done sharing the depths of myself with others and barely making ends meet. What once felt nourishing to my heart and soul—accessing my creative nature and expressing myself on stage—had become an energetic drain.

After completing our thru-hike and leaving the acting career behind, Daniel and I moved to Boston for no reason other than we both liked the city and figured it would be a fun place to live. With a recent gap in my resume and in the midst of a career change, I went to a temp agency and found myself starting a three-month job for a large international consulting firm. I didn't even know what a consultant was or did, but, apparently, I didn't need to in order to prove I could do the job. A few weeks in, my senior manager asked if I'd apply to work for the company permanently. I guess I had what it takes to be a full-time consultant after all. After finding a creative way to turn an acting resume into a business consulting resume (language can be a fascinating thing) and being flown to the company's Manhattan office, I ended up landing the position and shortly thereafter moving into a 250-square-foot apartment with my boyfriend in the Upper West Side of New York City. No, that's not a typo. It was the smallest space I've called "home" (other than the tent we'd used for six months while walking from Georgia to Maine).

It was the first (and only) time in my life I had a stable income and benefits, and, simultaneously, it opened me up to a life unlike what I had known before—traveling the country and the world, earning miles and hotel points, putting money away into stocks and savings and a 401k. Freedom and security all wrapped into one (or so it appeared). This was in stark contrast to the "starving artist" life of the first half of my twenties.

Over the course of the next four years, I'd relocated back to San Francisco, broken up with Daniel, moved into my studio, and quit my job. One of my mentors at the company saw my potential to do something more aligned and asked me to leave the company and join her on a project with a start-up. I let her confidence in me nudge me out of my comfortable and stable job (which wasn't all that hard to do, as the job felt very misaligned with my beliefs and values) and take a risk.

And a risk it was. Six months later, she and I both realized this new gig was even less aligned for me, given the founder of the start-up and his protege were selling an emotional intelligence training program while modeling very little of it themselves. I gave notice to my billionaire boss, who took the news really well and even flew me out to Chicago for a farewell dinner, and quit. With no Plan B. Again.

Now, nearly two years since I took one of the biggest leaps of my life, leaving my cushy corporate job, I still haven't found a way to make money sustainably while pursuing my calling. I have spent all my savings, cashed out my stocks and 401k, and am running out of space on my credit cards. It's interesting to notice how the past couple of years have called me to release all attachment to security—first from a job that paid well, then my "nest egg," now my home. It is as if the universe is really asking me to lean into every ounce (or dollar) of trust and surrender that I can muster.

Lucky for me, I have spent this time diving deep within myself, reading transformational books, taking a life coach training program, and teaching about mindfulness through my blog and videos. The experience has provided me with so much growth and expansion. Daily, I have practiced believing I am fully supported by the universe no matter what. Despite the challenges, I have deeply held onto the knowing that I am being aligned with my purpose, which includes authoring at least three books, no matter how long it takes. In so many ways, even though I am limited on resources, I feel so free. I have been committed to going within, creating loads of content, and sharing what I am learning with the world. I spend money as it feels aligned, even if it isn't in my bank account (my newly adopted definition of "financial freedom"). I have traveled when and where I want (and have always been supported to do so).

There have been so many moments when I've been unsure of what to do, and then I receive a sign or evidence to keep going or about which choice to make. For instance, when I walked away from my job and enrolled in a cult—I mean, a three-month development program—in New York, I wasn't sure how I'd afford it. I was on a flight back to San Francisco when I asked for guidance, and as soon as we landed and I turned on my phone, I had an Airbnb request from someone who wanted to rent out my apartment for the same three months I would be in Albany. This made it possible for me to afford to go. When I felt called to sign up for the life coach training program the following year and didn't have the $5,000 needed, I put aside my pride and asked my brother for help, which he quickly and generously offered. A few months later, I went to a women's retreat in Connecticut for said program. On the final day, one of the women facilitating a workshop mentioned she was hosting a trip to Peru for an Ayahuasca ceremony. I listened to the words she said without even knowing what they all meant, but something within me knew I must go. Without knowing any of the details or that this would cost me more than $10,000, I walked up to her after the workshop and said it was a "Hell, yes!" in my body to participate in this experience. Soon enough, with the help of my credit card, my boyfriend and I were on our way to Lima.

It seemed that when a desire arose, an answer followed. Periods of time spent traveling have been met with tenants willing to rent out my place for the exact amount of time that I would be gone, earning me enough money to cover my bills while away. Still, I was far from "thriving." I had learned about manifestation and the law of attraction in my life coach training program. If I got really clear on what I wanted to manifest, I would attract it into my life. I worked with this concept for a while. It was fun and exciting at first when I got clear that I wanted to see a hummingbird, and after seeing it appear first as a drink on a menu, I then saw one float directly in front of me at the park. Moral of the story: sometimes what we manifest comes in different forms and often when we're least expecting (so, not according to our timeline). If I can make a hummingbird appear, what else am I capable of? And why was the $20,000 I kept being clear about and envisioning and feeling deeply like I already had it not manifesting in my bank account?

Now, this book isn't about manifestation or the law of attraction. There is plenty of great content out there about that, and I'm not saying it's wrong or bogus. But I will say that this concept, which was all the craze during my time of transformation and exploration, eventually became a hindrance. I could feel that something about it didn't resonate with me. I mean, if I am the "creator of my reality" (whatever that really means), is the goal to be in full control of everything? Snap my fingers and watch it appear?

At the same time the law of attraction was making itself known to me, I read another influential book by Michael Singer, *The Surrender Experiment*. This story and example of how to live life resonated so much more with me. His practice, once he had his awakening, became saying "yes" to whatever life brought him. And his life unfolded in the most miraculous and mysterious and delightful ways. When I sat with this form of surrender compared to manifestation (which seemed to have very different energies about them), I determined neither was right nor wrong. Instead, I realized that we each get to choose how we play this game of life.

When it comes to me and my life circumstances, I haven't seen myself as a victim, but I also haven't seen myself as a conscious creator of my life, as someone who's in the driver's seat. You see, since the age of twenty-one, I have moved nine times in ten years. Only two of those times did I decide where to go by myself, of my own accord. I was always happy for my husband or boyfriend or company to decide for me. I didn't see my circumstances as happening *to* me (like some helpless pawn being moved around without its consent) nor happening *by* me (like the one moving the pieces). I saw what was happening as life putting me in places and offering me things that I probably wouldn't have chosen for myself had I been given the chance. It was my boyfriend's dream to hike the Appalachian Trail. Before that, I had never spent a night in a tent. I didn't know what a consultant even did, let alone dream of becoming one. Even life coaching was something a former colleague suggested I do. And Ayahuasca was a foreign word (literally and figuratively) that came out of nowhere.

Obviously, in each of these cases, I made the decision to say "yes," so you might say I was very much consciously choosing. But I moved through life with no strong preferences, someone who could easily "go with the flow," a person who was more interested in being guided than guiding. I'm not saying these perceptions or behaviors are wrong or bad. They are actually lovely characteristics. Some people spend their entire lives learning how to surrender to the flow of life. And I'm not suggesting this is some superior way of being or that I'm super evolved or highly enlightened or a master at surrendering. I have simply been too scared to choose a direction, instead allowing myself to be at sea without a sail. In this way, all I had to do was show up, say yes, and do the next thing.

Another time I said "yes" was when my college boyfriend of nine months asked me to marry him, and the word spontaneously made its way across my lips. Faced with a major life decision at the age of nineteen years old, surprisingly, I didn't take much time to consider my answer. I was married within two years' time and moved to California shortly thereafter. After three years of marriage, though, I felt trapped. I felt we weren't on the same page anymore. I fell in love with someone else. I felt like I had made the wrong choice. At twenty-four years old, I no longer wanted to be married to the man I had committed to spending the rest of my life with until "death do us part."

The amount of pain I felt, torn between upholding my commitment and listening to my heart's knowing, was excruciating, and I endured that pain for nearly a year, trying to make things work. How dare I pursue what I want after saying I would spend the rest of my life with someone? How dare I even feel those feelings or have those thoughts?! Eventually, I did the hard thing (though some—even myself—might say it was the easy thing, compared to staying in a relationship I no longer felt aligned with) and asked for a divorce. I knew I was breaking hearts. I knew I was hurting people. Still, I followed my heart's desire, as difficult as it was. Don't get the wrong idea here. It wasn't like one day I listened to what I deeply desired and then experienced everything I wanted—ultimate peace and freedom. I had chosen to trust myself, and it led to heartbreak. Why would I ever want to do that again?

In that moment of choosing to get a divorce, something much deeper, something I was unaware of, was happening. While I was letting go of one thing, I was becoming attached to a core belief that I had now proven once and for all—that I could indeed choose wrong and that I had done exactly that when I got married. Moreover, undoing this wrong choice was painful and hard.

From that point forward, I (unconsciously) decided it was unsafe to want something or someone specific or to follow my heart's desires and make choices based on them. After all, I might be wrong. It felt unsafe to commit to things lest I break my (or another's) heart or cause disappointment. Making a choice felt like it would trap me, imprison me, end up doing more harm, and create more suffering in my life. Even when it came to something as innocuous as ordering a meal at a restaurant, I struggled to make choices. What if I chose the wrong dish and was disappointed, or what if my heart was set on something and they didn't have it?! Since I was filled with so much doubt when I went to make a choice, I felt insecure making decisions. I felt "more secure" without a strong opinion of my own, letting others (or the universe) choose for me.

Perhaps manifestation works really well for some people. I mean, it must—look at all the thought leaders and teachers who speak about the subject and model its effectiveness. But it doesn't seem to work for me to get clear on one thing, focus all my awareness on it, and wait for it to appear. After trying that process, which has been disappointing and discouraging, I've realized that, for me, surrendering is the way to go. Through all of this, I feel I have been building a muscle to trust and have faith in something greater than myself, feeling more secure in that knowing in each and every moment. At the same time, I still feel insecure about the truth of who I am.

For as long as I can remember, I've been trying to "fix" those parts of me I've found to be unacceptable. I've spent my life exploring, searching, seeking out how to be the best version of myself, refusing to see how I am already enough. Many of these experiences have been deeply transformative and healing, giving me ample opportunities to dig into myself and look at parts I haven't always wanted to see. Now, in my thirties, I've been committed to learning more about myself and fully surrendering to the flow of life. In doing that, though, I've reached a point where it is too expensive and challenging to keep up with the cost of living in the place I've claimed as home.

After returning from Peru three months ago, I started to face some serious doubts. As much as I have wanted to believe that this new commitment to following my soul, being aligned with my purpose, and expanding myself to be less judgmental and more unconditionally loving would generate or magnetize what I need to survive and thrive in my life, it didn't seem to be happening. I was beginning to wonder why things in my life were not going the way I wanted or had thought they would by now. I have been experiencing what this newfound freedom looks and smells like—it certainly hasn't always been sunshine and roses—but I still couldn't understand why things still felt so hard and uncomfortable.

Finally, it came to a head. Frustrated that I felt I had to leave this beautiful city and place I loved so much, I began to question everything.

Maybe all this is a bunch of nonsense. Maybe I'm not meant to be a life coach or author after all. What am I doing? All the money and time and effort I'd been putting into myself for years now was feeling like a waste. I thought if I followed my path and did the next right thing, I (and the rest of humanity) would experience less pain and greater ease and flow. It's happening all around me. Entrepreneurs and coaches making six figures "effortlessly." Happy relationships in beautiful homes infiltrating social media. My life doesn't look like that. If there's one thing I've learned, it's to no longer ignore or judge those darker parts of myself but rather acknowledge them, build compassion for them, and even embrace them. Until I do, I can never be free. So, one day in the middle of packing up all of my things into a few boxes, hurt and confused, I did just that. And this is what spewed out onto my laptop.

What's the point? What does it even matter? We all go around wasting our time trying to figure this out. As if there is anything to figure out. It doesn't matter, so why even try? Look. I feel like shit. You feel like shit. We all feel like shit. Let's just get through this. Work. Eat. Watch TV. Fuck. And maybe read a book if you feel like it. I mean, this is what life is all about, right? Why overcomplicate it?

I'm sick of people trying to convince me there's a greater purpose. My purpose is to wake up every morning and do my best to survive. That's it. Done. I'm not here to make you feel good. I'm not here to save the children. I'm here because my parents fucked thirty-some years ago, and out I popped. I didn't ask to be here.

I'm sick and tired of wasting so much time and money on trying to improve myself. As if anyone out there knows what the fuck they're doing. And yet, here I am, throwing gobs of money at them to tell me how to live my life. Fuck that. I'm over it. I'm going to live my life how I want to live my life. It's my fucking life, after all. Meet the new fucking me.

Wow. There was a lot of anger and resentment bubbling up to be acknowledged and expressed. I've thought that I've been doing all the right things by being mindful and intentional and "aligned," but it doesn't seem to have made a difference. This part of me was so angry that all I got for listening to my inner knowing and trusting the flow of life was more uncertainty and insecurity.

I was beginning to wonder if, unlike Michael Singer, my practice of surrendering was just a way of keeping my ego safe. I perceived not making choices about things like where to go eat, where to live, what to do for a career, or who specifically I wanted to have as a life partner as a state of surrender when it was actually an act of fear. Fear that if I claim something (or someone or someplace) and then either my mind or something else changes, it will result in that same feeling of heartbreak all over again. What I've started to witness is we often manifest the very thing we fear in order to work through our fear of that thing. I mean, if I didn't get specific about what I wanted to manifest, it could go either way. I wouldn't end up disappointed or hurt. If I just went with the flow, I wasn't to blame if it didn't work out or if I changed my mind later. It kept me in this state of pseudo-non-attachment. Since I know that nothing lasts forever, I would unconsciously keep myself from feeling future pain, which only ended up creating more pain and suffering in the moment. Our minds have such a tricky way of keeping us safe.

For many years following my divorce, I feared commitment as something that felt threatening to my freedom (and not just when it came to people). I resisted committing to doing or not doing certain things in my life. My fear stemmed from a mistaken belief that commitment somehow overwrites the impermanent nature of life. If I commit to something, it means I can *never* change my mind or will *always* be in that situation. For example, if I make plans to do something, I *have* to do it, even if something shifts or I don't feel like doing it when the time comes. If I commit my heart to someone, I can *never* love another or feel differently. If I commit to live someplace, I will *always* live in that one place and nowhere else.

Now, what's funny is that I've disproved this theory of mine multiple times, including when I got married and divorced. Or when I committed to, first, my job as a consultant and, again, the start-up and then quit years (or months) later. And yet, even with this unfounded fear, I have still allowed myself to have this belief about commitment, creating greater conflict and tension and resistance to making decisions. This has continued through the years until I finally started to see it wasn't making the decision or committing to something that was "trapping" me. It was that I was misunderstanding, telling myself a story that wasn't true—that it was "safer" to *not choose.*

This belief has imprisoned me, especially as I take another leap of faith, leaving my home of many years. While I have known for a few months it is time to leave San Francisco, I have no idea what is next. My boyfriend and I have no obligations or reasons to move to any one particular place over another. I am faced with the freedom to go anywhere, do anything—and the myriad choices that go along with that. If I can live anywhere, how do I choose the "best" place to live? If I can do anything, how do I choose the "right" thing to do? Do we go to Seattle and stay with his sister, or Texas to see his mom, or South Dakota, where my parents live? Do we do a workaway in another country? There are no husbands or jobs or bucket-list adventures calling me to one place over another. This time, the choice is up to me.

With a sigh, I walk down the flight of stairs and uncomfortably climb into the driver's seat of my silver Toyota Corolla, packed with the only things I kept from the last decade of my life—three boxes' and two suitcases' worth. My boyfriend waits for me in the passenger's seat. We are quiet and a bit giddy as I turn left toward Market Street, my hand holding his, and drive east across the Bay Bridge.

As we approach I-80, I ask Michael, "So, north or south?" Ever wary of fucking things up, I want him to choose. For as much growing and inner work as I have already done, I am still holding onto a belief that I am vulnerable to some form of danger or threat based on the choices I make. I am still afraid my actions can and, therefore, will lead to disappointment or heartbreak. I am unsure of just how okay I will be, no matter what.

Michael contemplates my question for a moment. "South."

South it is. We will drive toward Los Angeles, contacting my cousin on the way to see if we can stop by and see her in Santa Barbara. We have a few friends in the L.A. area and are equally excited to check out other parts of Southern California. Maybe even make it to Mexico. Who knows? We have no home, no jobs, no agenda, no plan, and limited resources. We are footloose and fancy-free to do as we please and go where we want. And I feel bound by the constraints of that freedom.

CHAPTER 2

PURGING RESISTANCE

"Can you find out if he's single ... and straight?" I asked the bartender at one of my favorite go-to spots down the street from my apartment on the night I met Michael. The place was packed with people eating and drinking at the bar and high tops around me. I'd been eyeing this man at the end of the long mahogany bar, with dark hair, dark eyes, an infectious smile, and a perfect amount of stubble. I couldn't see who he was talking to, and given I lived in San Francisco, there was a decent chance he's gay. The bartender worked his magic, and moments later, this man was standing next to me, asking if I'd like to join him and his friends. By the end of the night, we made plans to see each other again in the coming days. Two years later, we're heading south together, unsure where exactly we'll end up.

From the start, at least in my relationships, I commit to being direct and putting myself, my desires, and my truth on the line with my partner. Thanks to some things I'd been learning about relationships and how to have the one I want, I told Michael after our first date what my non-negotiables are. He and I have been in agreement about practically everything—just not the "having a kid" part. But that's okay; I don't need one right now, and it is more important for me to be in partnership than to be a mother. So, I've swept that under the rug, along with a few other things.

I immediately fell in love with this man for who he truly is, seeing the divine in him. Early on, I realized he has an issue with alcohol, but for many months, I didn't know the extent of that. After hemming and hawing, still afraid of making the wrong choice, I decided to stick it out. And I continue to, knowing that this relationship, as challenging as it may be, is an opportunity for me. I get to practice non-judgment and acceptance of what is. Every. Single. Day.

Some people sign up for marathons to train themselves mentally and spiritually. I get into relationships. I know I consciously signed up for partnership with an alcoholic because of what I felt it would teach me and how it would expand me. Of course, this doesn't come without plenty of strife. It feels like I'm training for the Unconditional Love Olympics, and, boy, do I want to place amongst the top! To put it simply, this is one of the most loving and infuriating relationships I've ever had. I said "yes" to this opportunity and saw it as something the universe put on my path for a reason, and I am going to make the most of it.

I have made quick work of what the universe handed me. I constantly use our relationship as a way to practice being more accepting, more loving, more compassionate, and more patient. Please don't misunderstand me: these are incredible things, but by no means am I some perfect partner or Mother Teresa. I make plenty of mistakes. I get angry. I enable him. I continuously feel confused about what I ought to do or if I am doing the right thing. But this is a necessary part of my journey in order to prepare me for what could come next.

Steering the car south, I start getting into my head, reflecting on our time together as Michael flips through his phone. From the beginning, it's been important for me to love him enough for him to become the man I desire him to be. Soon into our relationship, I saw that this was an impossible task. I realized my love alone can't "heal" him, yet I desperately wanted him to heal. So, a few months ago, I invited him to go to Peru with me for the Ayahuasca ceremony I had felt called to attend. I was confident that Grandmother Medicine would do the trick and reveal to him what needed to be revealed for his highest good and ultimate healing. Then, he would be able to provide me with the things I need, and I could have the relationship (and child) I truly desire.

Trust me, I get how this sounds. It isn't as Machiavellian as you might think. My intentions were good. It was part of me exploring what it means to be the creator of my reality, and if I do a certain thing a certain way, I might actually get what I want when I want it. I could see and feel who he truly is—he simply wasn't yet aware of it, and I believed I could help. I've been clear on what I want to create for myself when it comes to partnership and family, but I can't fully accept that everything has its own timing, its own cycle, its own part to play in our lives.

And anyway, I didn't travel over 4,000 miles to spend ten days amidst the mountains in the Sacred Valley solely to heal Michael (and I sincerely knew that may not even be an outcome, but it didn't keep me from hoping). My intention going into ceremony was to honor all parts of myself that I tend to suppress or dismiss and let go of anything that keeps me from expressing those parts (shame, guilt, fear). I had spent the past few years reading about and practicing the concepts of non-judgment, non-resistance, and non-attachment. I had been actively learning that when we accept ourselves—wholly, just the way we are—and accept *all* parts of ourselves, we are free to experience the fullness of who we are, unencumbered by fear or worry or anxiety. Free from pretzeling ourselves as we avoid certain things or limit ourselves based on fearful beliefs or unhealed traumas. Yet, I have struggled to embody this. Sometimes, I even found myself questioning or misunderstanding what I'd been learning.

In November 2015, three months before I packed up my belongings for this trip, Michael and I sat with seven other individuals for our first of two Ayahuasca ceremonies on the full moon. Two days prior, we all journeyed together for nearly twelve hours with San Pedro, a heart-opening cactus used for hallucinogenic and healing purposes. For this next ceremony, we all gathered together in the maloca on our shaman's property, set in the valley between two large mountain ranges, known as "apus" in the local language. The scent of sage and palo santo filled the space. The sound of drums, rattles, and Icaros filled our ears. I could see the night sky through the round glass ceiling above as I lay on the mat dedicated for me in our circle. When my turn came, I was invited to get up and kneel in front of the shaman, and he presented me with the thick, dark brew. The taste was horrific, but the journey was exquisite.

Eckhart Tolle talks about three ways from which to do anything, what he calls "modalities of awakened doing"—acceptance, enjoyment, or enthusiasm. Acceptance is the most basic of all of these and what we can practice most often. We may not enjoy the taste of something or the frustration of dealing with an intoxicated person, but we can accept it. We may not feel enthusiastic about puking our guts out or looking at our shadows, but we can accept it.

I have resisted accepting what is for most of my life, constantly wishing things were different from what they are. Constantly dwelling on past mistakes and worrying about future mishaps. Constantly judging myself for what I am or am not doing. And constantly thinking that the present moment (and my present self) isn't enough.

Sometimes, I catch myself asking, "How can I possibly have the life I want if I settle for accepting what is? Isn't that just being passive? Won't I become even more lazy or apathetic than I already am?" Almost as if some part of me is saying, "If I accept what is (traveling around with my alcoholic boyfriend while our resources run out, unsure where we are going next), how will I ever be happy? Is it true that happiness only comes by avoiding or resisting this moment?"

What I've been learning, though, is acceptance isn't "stuffing down" or ignoring the situation. It involves acknowledgment of the situation, person, feeling, or what have you—not ignorance. Acceptance does not mean we don't act or respond. Quite the contrary, we respond to each moment precisely how it asks us to respond without the ego getting in the way and reacting or judging or creating drama. Accepting that it's time to move can still mean taking action to pack my bags. Accepting that my partner has a dysfunctional relationship with alcohol can still mean I respond to it.

There is a lovely story of a Chinese farmer who lived his life according to the mantra "Maybe." He responded to good news and bad news alike in total acceptance of (non-resistance to) the moment. At each step in the farmer's journey, he responds to whatever the present moment asks of him without drama or suffering. Acceptance does not lead to apathy (as I feared it might). Acceptance leads to peace.

I would have glimpses of these insights in my day-to-day life, but it was with the help of Ayahuasca that I began to understand them in a much deeper way on a cellular level. This psychedelic Amazonian vine is known to offer the recipient the exact experience that individual needs or asks for. So, I wasn't surprised that the major themes that made themselves known to me during my plant medicine journeys were radical self-acceptance and self-responsibility.

On the first night, Grandmother showed me, using my own inner wisdom, that I do not know anything from my mind. It's my intuition that knows all, as it is fed from the source of the universe and all divine knowledge. This was simultaneously upsetting and freeing. I knew this was a key piece of information being delivered to me for my awakening process. Still, I was surprised by how gentle she was with me (all things considered). I had been so afraid of what I might encounter on the journey—all the darkness and horrible things I am capable of. Instead, I was shown just how powerful and beautiful and incredible I am. This newfound awareness became a new foundation for me as I began the slow and steady process of freeing myself from beliefs that keep me stuck out of fear.

As I was well into the journey, I made my way to the bathroom, crawling on my knees and using my hands to help me find the way, as it was quite dark and I was quite under the influence of the medicine. As I returned to the space on my knees, I heard a voice tell me to get up and walk. I ignored it out of fear that others might think I was showing off by being able to stand upright and not fall over. I felt I needed to remain on my hands and knees lest I disturb others or seem overly confident. By the time I had nearly reached my mat, the voice returned, commanding me to turn around, go back, and walk to my mat this time. I begrudgingly listened. I successfully did so without disturbing a single person. It felt amazing. What I later realized is that no one was even paying attention to me and what I was doing—they were each having their own journey. It also showed me just how capable I am.

Back on my mat, I had a vision of Michael and me having a child, and it dawned on me that expressing this desire is something I've suppressed out of fear. Fear that I'll lose Michael if I pursue that desire. Fear that I won't be able to get pregnant. Fear that I will lose the life I currently know. Fear that I couldn't have both a family *and* pursue doing my work in the world. Fear that if I want a child badly enough, I'll experience disappointment or, worse, devastation by having that desire (or another one) taken from me. Experiencing this fear and its limiting beliefs so deeply was both beautiful and painful.

Grandmother worked with my inner wisdom to show me something else I judge and suppress out of fear of being abandoned: my "neediness." Even the fact that I label it that way is telling. There are times in my life (as there are for each one of us) when I'm "needy," but that's not good or bad; it just is. Yet I have carried a lot of shame around this for most of my life, whether from experiences as a child or because it was written in the stars as part of my astrology (or, probably, all and none of that at the same time). As an adult, it has translated to not being able to feel comfortable asking for what I need in a relationship or in life. I, at times, repress speaking (or even feeling) my desires for fear that I would then be seen as "needy," which means I am not whole and complete in and of myself. It means I'm a burden on others. It means I'll push people away. It means I've most likely done something wrong to be in a place where I'm incapable of providing for myself all that I want and desire.

During the ceremony, I felt a shift and a newfound acceptance of this part of me and how essential it is to need others and things beyond myself. After all, all of life and nature are interdependent. Trees need nutrients from the soil and energy from the sun. Bees need pollen, and flowers need bees. Why would it be any different for humans? We are not designed to provide all things for ourselves. We are intended to rely on one another to complete the picture, to fill in the gaps.

Growing up, though, I saw the dysfunction of codependency, which so many of us suffer from. In an attempt to experience life differently, especially when it comes to romantic relationships, I have swung in the opposite direction—toward independence, supporting myself (and sometimes, the other), afraid of being dependent on anyone. The thing is, that's impossible, so it has become a limiting belief I've simply attempted to dance around. A suppressed fear that has often been expressed in a dysfunctional way, like in overgiving and struggling to receive. Caught up in this dance, I have found myself in the greater part of the past decade more in my masculine energy trying to lead than in my feminine energy willing to follow, doing whatever I could to prove how capable and resilient and strong I am while repressing my own needs.

To this very day, I notice how many people still avoid the words "need" and "needy" like they're dirty. It's as though we have collectively been programmed or taught that it isn't okay to need people or things. We even get clever and replace the word with "want" or "desire." And that's okay. Sometimes, it is a want or desire. But, sometimes, it is a need. And that is also okay.

The fear of needing someone or something has permeated our culture, and it leaves us falsely believing that we can make it on our own. It casts shame and blame on those who might have more needs or are more willing to express those needs. At the end of the day, we all need things. Some of us need different things than others. A palm tree might need something different than an oak tree, and we don't wrong one over the other. We don't shame a dog for needing something different than a cat needs. If one of us needs a relationship, there is nothing wrong with that. If one of us needs money, there is nothing wrong with that. If one of us needs freedom, there is nothing wrong with that. If one of us needs security, there is nothing wrong with that. And, in turn, what we each have to give satisfies a need of someone else.

During my second six-hour Ayahuasca journey, I noticed how, similar to neediness, I often judge control as a bad thing and am afraid of "being controlling." Now sometimes, control can indeed be tyrannical or overbearing. But true power is not found in having power *over* others. We often control things because we desire a particular outcome, which isn't even often within our control, or because we don't like what's happening. Control in and of itself isn't negative, but I feared it as such because I assumed if I was "in control," I was manipulating someone (by the way, another neutral word that's gotten a bad rap).

Swimming in the sea of consciousness that was available to me through the medicinal effects of the hallucinogenic brew, I realized I *do* control things—we all do—starting with making each moment what it is. I choose how to experience each of those moments, and I choose how to respond to each experience. In ceremony, I was able to notice how this is often done through my breath, and instead of judging my experience as "bad," I became aware that it just is. My breath helped me control whether or not I felt sick or whether or not I was in the present moment. Instead of seeing this form of control as something wrong, I was able to see it as an act of radical self-responsibility in each moment. It is a practice I have taken with me into my life and that has left me pondering, what's the difference between controlling my reality and creating it? My medicine journey (much like my life) was my creation; my experience was my own doing. It was not anyone else's.

As the medicine continued to work through me, I was shown how feelings of blame in my life have touched my relationships, most recently with Michael, whom I had been unconsciously blaming (and whose alcoholism I blamed) for my grief and my feeling that ours isn't an ideal relationship. While I was clear about his contribution to my experience, in that same moment, I felt what it's like to take full responsibility for choosing him and co-creating the relationship and his alcoholism. It was so freeing to see how I created it for my own experience and growth and how I have contributed to it. I felt so much love and compassion for him and myself in that moment.

Turning onto the exit for Highway 1, I look over at Michael, now taking a nap. I am aware of how easily I can let myself get into fearful or worrisome thoughts, like how long I have before he starts drinking or if I have what it takes to love him through this. Self-responsibility means knowing in each moment that we choose our existence or our reality—I choose how I feel, how I respond, what I believe, what I *don't* believe. As we begin to take full responsibility and get out of our victim mindset (which the ego just loves!), we lighten our load and begin to experience our true power. And with great power comes great responsibility. If we are going to influence or direct the course of our lives, we need to remember that we are responsible for all of it. We must be willing to take responsibility for our thoughts, feelings, actions, and behaviors and let go of the ones no longer serving us. Of course, this can be a lot harder than it sounds. And when we don't, we go around the world causing more damage, pointing fingers, triggering others—perpetuating cycles of pain. Hurt people hurt people.

Being responsible for my reality goes hand-in-hand with the practice of non-attachment, letting go, releasing. When partaking in plant medicine, especially Ayahuasca, it is very common to purge (or puke) after consuming it. It is said that what we purge is what the body is ready to release on an energetic level. It is a clearing and a cleansing of the toxic thoughts, behaviors, and beliefs we may carry with us. When I began vomiting underneath the bright stars shining down on the Sacred Valley, it was very clear to me what I was releasing. The first time I did, I released my need for control (not the act of it, but its self-limiting patterns and beliefs). The second time, I purged my judgment, which, as a tool that helps me discern and navigate things in my life, often prevents me from accepting things. More than that, I was releasing the judgment I have of my judgment.

What blew my mind was finding that the point isn't letting go of the pattern or behavior (though sometimes the pattern may no longer occur) but, rather, letting go of my resistance to it. It is only by accepting all parts of ourselves, including the patterns we typically judge or resist, that we can let go of trying to change them. We first have to look at them and experience them non-judgmentally, and then they can fall away. Or, as Eckhart Tolle says, "Egoic patterns, even long-standing ones, sometimes dissolve almost miraculously when you don't oppose them internally." Through this purging, it was as if my resistance to these struggles was what I was letting go of.

While the two San Pedro ceremonies and two Ayahuasca ceremonies spread out over eight days didn't heal Michael, they showed me more clearly how to be okay with who I am, free of judgment, and in greater acceptance. Thanks to the experience, I now tell myself, "I'm okay" or "That's okay" whenever I have an opportunity to judge myself. Acceptance is the foundation for learning to love exactly who you are and where you are in this very moment.

I offer a cautionary use of the words "who you are"—the ego is quick to think it knows exactly who you are. What I am referring to is the deeper, truer version of yourself. During the very cerebral experience of this medicine journey, I felt this on a cellular level for the first time in my life. I viscerally experienced all the times I would go into my head in response to what I was doing (controlling the moment or keeping myself from feeling a certain way), recognize the judgment taking place there, and instead choose to feel acceptance throughout my entire being. This was a turning point for me as I started to deeply understand how it feels to be in total acceptance. By truly accepting what is (as opposed to judging or resisting), one can fully let go and be in alignment with the flow of the universal order of things.

Much like misunderstanding acceptance, I have struggled with what it means to practice non-attachment. What in the world does this mean? How do I let go? What does that look like? It seems like a very active process. Like a cutting off or a dropping. Does this mean I can't hold onto anything at all? Not want anything? Not desire anything? These are some of the first questions I ask myself when Michael, stirring from his nap, asks if he can get a beer for the road and I feel the frustration arise within me. Am I not allowed to desire him to make better choices? Must I be non-attached to every choice he makes? But then I am reminded of how Grandmother taught me that we cannot force ourselves to let go of something or release attachment to it (that very thought or practice is often rooted in resistance). I can't force myself not to care how Michael behaves or how that impacts me. I can't force myself to let go of my desire to have a partner who doesn't continuously numb out or forget who he is.

Resistance is our attempt to rid ourselves of the unacceptable. We believe that if we don't accept something, it won't happen (or we can keep it from happening again). Sometimes, we even believe that if we *do* accept it, it won't happen again. This is a sneaky way to sidestep true acceptance. Either way, we are resisting what is.

Why do we continue to delude ourselves into thinking that pretending something doesn't exist or pushing against it will somehow cause it to disappear? Because the alternative seems scarier. We think that if we don't at least pretend something will go away, the alternative is to welcome it into our lives. We fear that we, in some way, will give the impression that we are okay with the pain and suffering and heart-ache in our world (and within ourselves). I faced this when I accepted that I am in love with an alcoholic—what does that mean about me? If I accept that within me (and in the world at large), what am I to do with all that? So, I stay in the illusion of keeping bad things at bay. This can come in the form of avoidance, distraction, indulgence in things I would rather experience, and, my favorite, trying to figure it out so as to ensure it never happens again.

What I am learning is that it is only by accepting everything as it is (which requires being in non-judgment) that non-attachment can occur as a byproduct. Letting go is a non-action. It is what occurs when we no longer resist something (by pushing or pulling). It is allowing whatever will be to be. And in this allowance, in this surrender, we are no longer clenching our fists. Instead, we face our hands up and hold it in our palms. There is no gripping; there is simply letting it be there. Then and only then can we release our attachment to a specific outcome or, as Alan Watts would say, avoid getting stuck.

The more we practice acceptance, the more we start to see how things happen just the way they are meant to. We are letting things be, which doesn't require any additional effort; it simply requires surrender. We are practicing what the Taoists and Zen Buddhists refer to as "mushin," or "no mind," which can also be interpreted as non-choosing. In order to free oneself to choose and, therefore, live without hesitation, we must step beyond duality. Much like how I witnessed Michael do when he quickly proclaimed "south," almost as if he wasn't choosing at all. Stepping into non-duality, seeing that no one choice is "better" than another, we can let go of the fear that so often stops us in our tracks and see that everything is mutually arising, two sides of the same coin.

Whether or not it involves reincarnation or past lives, a single lifetime is made of many journeys. It's like a continuous spiral—we keep going around and around and around, seeing things from different perspectives as we "climb" or "move forward." Of course, we know this isn't linear and there aren't some kind of hierarchical levels to this sort of journey. But my point is, we will experience many hero's journeys if we choose to answer the call. At this stage of my journey to becoming free, I am being asked to start by letting go of the beliefs that have led me to behave as though there *is* a right and wrong way of doing just about anything.

In the Sacred Valley, I experienced a profound level of transformation unlike any I'd had before, but it isn't like flipping a switch and immediately integrating or embodying all that I now know. Hearing Michael laugh lovingly as he shares a text message his friend sent with me, I am reminded of when my shaman laughed compassionately when I told him about the funeral I had for my ego during my first San Pedro journey. I felt so proud to have finally released this unacceptable part of me and put her to rest. This part of me who had improper desires or behaved in inappropriate ways or kept me from being all that I am here to be. He knew what I would only later realize—it doesn't work that way. There is no burying the ego once and for all.

CHAPTER 3

COMING UNDONE

The way the ocean meets the land along Pacific Crest Highway is stunning. With no place to be or schedule to follow, Michael and I take the scenic route down the coast. Our new adventure awaits us. Faith and freedom, here we come! Over the course of the next many weeks, we find ourselves staying with family and friends in Southern California before making our way to Baja, where I finally start making real progress on my first book, *Becoming Enough*.

I spend the days reflecting on what I have learned over the past few years and, more specifically, over the past few months since journeying with plant medicine. For more than a year now, I have been turning my experiences into videos and blogs and workshops to share with others. Doing so, I process the transformation I am going through, and I continue doing that from each location and mood I find myself in, whatever that may be.

Traveling around, free as a bird, following my dreams, being in the flow of life, doing what so many others wish they could do—the reality is, it's really hard at times. With all the inner work I'm doing (and thinking I left my ego in Peru), I thought it would feel easier. For heaven's sake, just three months earlier, I returned from one of the most transformational experiences of my life. Instead, I find myself often frustrated—with my partner, with my circumstances, with myself. I am on a journey to living a life with less judgment, resistance, and attachment, but I have a long way to go. I may not belittle myself or agonize over doing things as I once did, but I am certainly experiencing how easy it is to get stuck at various steps along the way.

Michael and I have been on the road for a couple of months and find ourselves at an Airbnb in Rosarito. We are faced with a tough decision. We are running out of money, and things aren't lining up as we had hoped. I can't tell if I am being guided to step into greater faith and stay here in Mexico, trusting that all will be provided, or to let my bank account balance cut our trip short. As much as I hate to admit it, I realize I have no way of knowing how things will turn out in the future. Maybe we are being guided to stay, and maybe we aren't. Suddenly, there are so many thoughts running through my head about how I really don't know anything. I realize that one minute, I'm talking about how amazing things are and how things unfold so easily and effortlessly when I'm in a state of flow, and then the next minute, it's like I have to take all that back or at least acknowledge that I really don't know how anything works. It brings up a common question I ask myself: "Am I being faithful or foolish?" I wonder if believing that I am always provided for, or the "universe has my back," is demonstrating trust or naiveté. For example, if I have a few hundred dollars in my bank account and then trust I'll receive more, is it an act of faith or foolishness to not get a job? Or is it foolish to spend money on things versus a demonstration of faith that money is always there when I need it?

Uncertainty is a major theme in my life. As much as I enjoy the flexibility and spontaneity, I desire more than anything to know what's coming next and have a plan. I feel so unsettled not having that. I hate the feeling of not knowing what's next or not knowing how this all works. It brings tears to my eyes because I just don't know, and I want to so badly. How am I supposed to live when I don't know? And if I don't know, what does that mean? Well, it means that I have no direction or purpose. It means that I'll make a mistake, that I'm a fraud, bad things will happen to me, I am abandoning myself, I won't have the life

I want, and I'll forever feel stuck and unhappy. Wow. Well, that took a turn. But this is what it's like living inside my head. You're welcome.

Ultimately, we decide not to stay in Mexico. I'm sad, disappointed, a little ashamed. I wonder if we are giving up too soon, unwilling to have faith for it to work out. I can see that I am attached to the idea of living in another country and writing a book. I guess it's not going to look like that—at least not right now, and maybe not ever. Oh, well. I wonder if part of non-attachment also means accepting the unacceptable, knowing that there will always be unacceptable aspects to nature. We drive back to our friend's place in Southern California to figure out our next move.

After some deliberation, Michael and I decide to drive to my childhood home of Sioux Falls, South Dakota. We head that way, stopping in Las Vegas to celebrate my birthday in early March, where Michael drunkenly proposes to me one night in a bar. To this proposal, I say "no." We plan to stay with my parents for a few months as we regroup, earn some money, and get our feet back under us. Moving home, I have the opportunity to take a long, hard look at myself.

My intention of moving home is to create a sense of security, to relieve some pressure and have the time and space to finish my book (I may not have an ocean view here, but it turns out that writing a book may still happen). When I contemplate what security feels like, it feels like being able to relax. And that's exactly what I do at home with my parents, at least in some ways. I rest. I stop pushing and striving so hard. It gives me time to learn how to pause and create more time to listen.

Free from having to pay rent or feeling afraid I won't have a place to sleep or food to eat, I'm able to do a lot of writing and inner reflection, seeing where I am still stuck in areas of my life. I'll be honest—it feels like quite the low point to move back in with my parents at the age of thirty-four, broke, and with my boyfriend who is often drunk, which leaves him in and out of work (and jail). It is definitely not my proudest moment. Still, I make the best of it (or, perhaps, it makes the best of me). Sometimes, it takes falling on my face to remind me that I'm not here to do it alone. None of us are.

Living across the hall from my parents offers me many opportunities to feel all sorts of things. Here I am, aspiring for the gold medal in what it means to accept what is and let go of my attachments, and I am feeling so discouraged. Despite my alignment and efforts, I am not reaching the number of people I want to reach, whether through my videos or the podcast I just started, or making money in exchange for my gifts, and my boyfriend continues to get drunk nearly every day. I want to hire a mentor, but I don't have the money. I want to move into my own place, but I don't have the money. I want to do a lot of things that feel aligned, but I don't have the money.

Most days, I find myself asking a series of questions. Am I being lazy? Why don't I try harder? If only I worked harder, life wouldn't be so painful, things would be easier, and I would have what everyone else has. Yet this goes against everything I have been practicing and sharing with others—being good with being me, doing less and being more. I begin to wonder if my entire message, my entire construct, my entire way of *being* in this world and everything I share with others is actually a scam and *not* true. These doubts, while a natural part of the process (especially as I'm preparing to share my truth in the form of a book), rock my world. They also serve a very valuable purpose.

I attempt to understand these qualities I observe about myself. I initially assume they are sabotaging me and that they aren't part of who I truly am. I find that I am so focused on evolving myself that I'm unwilling to accept these qualities—truly accept them—for what they are: a part of me. We all, at times, are lazy, complacent, disappointing. I realize I am stuck believing I can change parts of myself by feigning acceptance when, deep down, I still find parts of who I am unacceptable.

One day, listening to a podcast as I take a walk around my parent's neighborhood, I hear the host, Jody England, talking about how we are all shackled to different things and coming "undone." I am compelled to see where I am still in these shackles and where I am learning to free myself. Where am I keeping myself chained to the cell wall? Where am I coming undone? She reminds me how we're all at different places and need different things, which is why this is a lifelong practice. Throughout life, we continue the process of seeing where we're stuck, keeping ourselves unfree. In keeping with my typical nature—reflective, investigative, curious—I begin to explore a number of beliefs I am attached to.

I awake one morning with my familiar thoughts of sadness and guilt, feeling like I am "failing at life." I mean, to many people's standards (including my own), I am. As usual, I go to my self-improvement toolbox and ask myself one of Byron Katie's questions: "Is it true?" If you're not familiar with her work, it can be very supportive, though very mental. At this point in my life, I know that the stories behind my feelings aren't true, but it sure feels like they are. I'm beginning to realize that trying to break free from them using my mind is like using a flat iron to smooth rough water.

I notice my feelings of inadequacy, anger, and deep sadness. If I could just figure this out, surely I wouldn't feel this way. Is it because my partner is struggling or because I haven't yet released something I need to release? Have I not been taking care of myself, eating well, exercising? Am I out of alignment? I am so tired of breaking each and every thing down, looking for the answer. These questions are driving me crazy. Suddenly, I interrupt my "need to know" and simply feel the feelings. I go for a jog, allowing my body and the energy to move.

The next morning, I awake feeling very different. I don't have those thoughts of failure or inadequacy. I don't feel like crying or moping or screaming. I notice that it's a new day, completely different from the one before, even if my circumstances are the same. While in meditation, I am reminded once again that everything comes and goes—nothing is permanent.

If that is so, then trying to pin down and analyze why I feel a certain way in a given moment is a little silly, I suppose, like trying to pinpoint the exact location of something that is undoubtedly going to move. What if I simply acknowledge these thoughts and reactions as they arise and go about my day? Yes, I have doubts. That's interesting. Oh, I feel sad. Nothing to become attached to. God, I'm angry. Nothing to fear. Just let it float by like clouds passing in the sky. What if these feelings didn't mean something? What if they are just that—feelings—and I no longer need to go to the source of them? I have spent my life (at least many, many years) trying to understand why I am the way I am through self-help books. I have gotten to the root of my thoughts and feelings by doing inner work, like inner child work and neural linguistics programming, and just about anything my life coach training program taught me. I have worked with a therapist, trying to uncover what lies underneath it all, including trauma and unprocessed shame and anger. For a long time, I've thought I need to understand in order to heal. Now, I'm at a place in my journey where I am beginning to realize that is actually where I am getting stuck.

Being with my feelings, neither avoiding nor denying them, helps them move through me and be released. But understanding where they come from or why they're there isn't entirely necessary. I mean, it's one thing when we're still healing trauma or going into our past to reveal and release old wounds or patterns, but I've done so much of that already.

I realize something more insidious is happening. My need to know has stopped serving as a tool and is now a weapon. I see how shackled I am to the need to examine and, therefore, fix parts of myself. And I'm exhausted. I want to just *be* and stop thinking all the time. Still, I fear that thinking all the time might, in fact, be "who I am." Am I to embrace it and surrender to it? If I do, what good would come of that? (See what I mean? I can't shut it off.) In addition to overthinking and trying to figure things out, it seems that I'm also shackled to *not* being good with being me.

And what if I do "figure it out"? Do I think that I'll figure out a way to never feel hurt or guilt or failure or inadequacy or sadness or anger ever again? What's wrong with feeling that way, anyway? Well, I don't like how it feels. It doesn't feel good. I don't like who I am when I feel that way. Okay, and yet, all of that is judgment and resistance. This is what's keeping me stuck, believing I can figure out why I feel a certain way so I can avoid feeling it in the future. In reality, I have been avoiding the unacceptable nature of being human.

But being human *can't* be avoided, and all feelings are a part of that experience. It's all about how we relate to the pain we feel. It seems that the more we study the human condition, the more we think we can outsmart it. There's nothing wrong with figuring things out or understanding how things work, so long as we don't believe that doing so will cause them to stop happening. We can understand why a flower withers, but that doesn't mean it will stop dying. We can understand why hurricanes occur, but that doesn't keep them from occurring. We can understand where our pain and suffering come from, but that doesn't mean they will cease to be.

I can't outwit being human. As hard as I push, I can't push hard enough to get past that discomfort (yes, I see the paradox here). Trying to avoid the pain or figure it out just creates more. I have thought that if I just resist or struggle or push hard enough, I would "arrive" and no longer feel this way. What I'm realizing is that acceptance (like letting go) doesn't require effort. The effort is found in the resistance to what is—whether that be my life circumstances or the discomfort I'm feeling in the moment. Equally, acceptance doesn't mean not doing anything at all; it is a conscious and active state of being.

I think of yoga, a practice that has been such a wise teacher for me, and how it allows me to make sense of my experience of life in a very tangible way. It helps me take mental constructs and bring them into my body, into the physical realm. While attending a class one day, the instructor reminds us that the place to be is in our soft edge—not too comfortable but not too painful. This is where we see change and growth. I love this as a metaphor for life! And I see this as the sweet spot so many of us are seeking in our lives. A thought pops into my head: "Amanda, didn't you create this life for yourself so that you can practice accepting who you are and what you have despite the discomforts you might experience? If life was already perfectly painless, would you get to practice this way of being? Would you find your life's path? Embody your soul's contract? Would you learn to be good with being you, just the way you are?" The life I've chosen feels intertwined with this process, but being good with being me doesn't always feel amazing, and it certainly hasn't been effortless.

For quite some time, I have had this belief (many of us do) that in order to be growing and receiving the benefits of the pose (aka life),

I need to be struggling, breathing hard, or really uncomfortable. (I imagine this is why I was so drawn to Bikram yoga for so many years.) I have experienced this both on and off the mat and am hyper-aware of it now that I am having the opportunity to reset and relax at my parent's house, which provides both comforts and discomfort, like being compressed with my boyfriend into a bedroom just across the hall from them for months by this point.

I start to consider that I can hold a pose, breathe into it as well as the shaking muscles and slight discomfort, and still experience a sense of flow and ease. Equally, just because I am in the flow of life doesn't mean I don't experience some discomfort or doubt. There can be discomfort in ease and ease in discomfort. Sometimes, I can relax deeper into the discomfort; other times, I pull back just a bit to create more ease. It's about finding balance, and I get to choose in each moment. To be simultaneously with the ease and the discomfort—not pushing it away or creating more of it unnecessarily—is allowing it to be in flow.

I can, in fact, maintain life's poses while flowing with and breathing into the discomforts that arise (like not knowing how I'm going to pay off my credit card debt or if I should break up with my partner or what life might surprise me with next), while simultaneously pulling back a bit before I tear something (by not pushing so hard or overthinking things). I have learned how my imagination is so often worse than reality (something Grandmother showed me in ceremony). I can sit with the discomfort while remaining open to what miracles might happen. And, despite how hard it is at times, I can soften a bit more and have faith that all will work out. It might just look different from what I had spent the last few months (or years) imagining.

CHAPTER 4

LEARNING TO RECEIVE

One summer morning, over a cup of coffee and the clattering of mugs at a local coffee shop, a new friend and mentor shares a story of a boat that can go up to seventy miles per hour on the open ocean. Pretty unheard of. One day, Clint recalls, they went to push back from the dock and turned on the engines, but the boat went nowhere. Two 300-horsepower engines at full throttle, and the boat didn't move. Then, someone noticed they hadn't been unanchored. An anchor the size of my friend's head (maybe fifteen pounds) was pulled in. Sometimes, he explains, even the smallest anchors keep us stuck.

As Clint tells me this story, tears stream down my face. I think about Michael. Is he my anchor? It's easy to point to a specific person, especially a partner, and cast the blame on him, even after everything Ayahuasca had revealed to me. But then, I begin to wonder if I, with my beliefs and fears, am my own anchor.

As a child, I believed I could figure out the "right" way to be human. Then, as I got older, I figured the pain and suffering I experienced meant I'm not good enough. As if the reason things feel hard or uncomfortable is because of my own doing or the people I'm surrounding myself with or the fact that I'm "goofing off" (aka enjoying myself or listening to my body) rather than getting serious about creating what I desire.

There is a common misconception that we are in control of this thing called life, that if we just get our alignment or energy "right," we can have everything the heart desires and avoid what it doesn't. But this still assumes there's a right way and a wrong way—so, once again, I must be doing it wrong! Some part of me still can't help but believe that it is because I am "out of alignment" that my life isn't unfolding as I want. I'm doing flow wrong. I'm doing manifestation wrong. I'm doing enlightenment wrong. I'm obviously not doing enough work on myself, and my external reality is reflecting that back to me.

If I am in love with an alcoholic, living with my parents, broke, and unable to build a six-figure business, I obviously haven't earned a better life and am, therefore, still unworthy of what I want—healthy partnership, money, my dream house, a child. If only I did it "right," then things would be comfortable and in flow. Right? Yet, this still assumes that life flows smoothly. Here's the thing. So long as I continue to believe there is one particular way to do things in order to have what I want, I live from the belief that there are two sides—"this is good and okay" versus "that is bad and not okay"; "this is aligned" versus "that is not aligned."

After having recorded more than a dozen podcast episodes for my "Being Inspired Radio Show," so much starts coming up for me around the duality of existence. The language is shifting, but it is still rooted in judgment and the belief that there is a "this" and a "that"—rather than a non-dualistic understanding that it all just is—and that I am to avoid one of them. As if I am to live a life that only has an upside and no downside. As if somehow I can climb a one-sided mountain or surf a wave that has no trough. And if I can figure out how to do that, I can earn the life I am here to live and prove myself worthy to have it. As if there is some particular version of existence I am meant to live, as opposed to whatever is happening being the life I am meant to live.

What if it's true that there is no alternative? That there is no other life I'm meant to have? Otherwise, it would be occurring. In some ways, this might assume there is no free will, something I go back and forth about. I suppose when I look at it, yes—we have choices, and those choices lead to consequences. Still, I can't ignore how those consequences or lessons somehow manage to be exactly what we need, part of our path and unfolding. How much free will does an oak tree have? I suppose it can bend toward the sun or grow taller above other trees, but it will always be an oak tree and have the exact experience it, as an oak tree, is meant to have.

Over the course of the last few months, I have spent a lot of time at a co-working space designed for entrepreneurs. When it comes to my work in the world, I'm often faced with wondering if I'm doing it right or "in the most aligned way" (as if this, too, is universal). Stepping out of the traditional workforce and creating a path for myself has opened me up to all sorts of input and opinions. And not just from those who thought I needed to get a "real job" but also from those paving their own paths and who figure they know best.

From the start, I have been clear about how I want to pursue my professional path, and it doesn't match a lot of what I've seen in terms of hustling or sales funnels or even the "spiritual" version of entrepreneurship and capitalism. I find that each step of the way, I am constantly needing to stay clear on what I know to be true for myself and what feels right and most aligned *for me*. I keep anchoring in my new belief: if I know the gifts I am here to contribute to the world and how I desire to do that, then that's my truth, and I can trust that. How and when that comes into form, who chooses to work with me or support me is out of my control. Those I'm meant to serve are also on their own journey.

At times, staying true to myself means not having much money in my bank account, so I wait some tables, do some catering, work as a ghostwriter and editor for a local publishing company, and even help out other entrepreneurial friends. But I stay committed to my integrity to myself as well as my intention and vision to write and publish my book, record my podcast, and become a transformational author, speaker, and thought leader.

I soon begin supporting a handful of other people with writing their books. While working on my own, I meet a woman at a women's gathering. She asks me what I do, and I respond assuredly, "I'm an author."

She just so happens to be an independent publisher who wants to help me bring my book into the world. We connect immediately, and I know we are meant to work together. But I don't have the money to hire her. Similar to how I felt when I wanted to hire a mentor, I am upset and discouraged. It's both frustrating and doesn't feel fair. I feel the limitations of money keeping me from following my dreams, forgetting how money has a way of appearing when I need it.

One day feels particularly hard. I cry. I want to give up, throw in the towel. I feel mad at the universe, spirit, source, whatever it is. In one week, I experience not one but two major disappointments. A woman hired me to help her write her book, and I've been overjoyed. She felt like a perfect fit and paid her first installment right away. A few days later, she tells me she didn't want to continue. I feel heartbroken. I have a hard time not thinking it's personal or that I've done something wrong. Then, to top it off, I have been putting into practice some of what I've been learning about manifestation (yes, I still give that a go from time to time). Many weeks back, I wrote myself a check with an exact amount I wanted to receive by a certain date, putting it in a special place and feeling into how I'd feel when I received that money and all that I would do with it. The day comes and goes, but that amount hasn't arrived—not even close. In turn, I find myself believing that who I am isn't worthy of success or even love (since this is where my mind tends to go). It feels like yet more evidence that I am being punished if I do (or don't do) certain things.

When something doesn't work out or I don't get what I ask for, I sometimes believe God (not some guy with a white beard, but the divine) is a malevolent force. Yet I know so deeply that all is happening *for* me, so it's hard to stay in that place of blame and defeat for long. Still, that is where the disappointment stems from—this need to have things go a certain way so I feel safe and loved. I start to see just how much I place my worth and value on what occurs outside of me.

In my typical response to feelings and reflections such as this, I pull out my laptop and start writing. I've learned over the years that we are channels and that wisdom can flow through us when given the opportunity. I'm often surprised by what is revealed to me when I have a dialogue with myself and type out the words I hear. It's often at my darkest moments when the greatest revelations occur. On this particular day, I engage in a dialogue between my wounded inner child, who really wants to throw a tantrum, and my higher wisdom. My inner child goes first.

"I'm sick and tired of being told to trust and listen and wait, and then nothing happens! I get my hopes up, and then it all comes crashing down around me! It's as if the universe or God or whatever is laughing at me as we speak. 'Look at her getting all excited as if she is somehow on the right path and totally supported. Let's just take it all away from her. Ha!' That's so mean. I hate it. I'm tired of holding an intention and thinking positive thoughts and letting go, and then when things don't go my way, learning to always see what's in it for me. When will it be my turn to experience the success and abundance and cash money everyone keeps talking about? Why is it always so much easier for everyone else?! I read the right books, meditate daily, listen to the right audios, receive transmissions, and am open to divine guidance. I'm doing everything I can, and still, I get the short end of the stick. This is bullshit. I'm sick of it. I know I'm amazing and have gifts to share and value to offer others. I know others are inspired by me. So, why can't I experience what everyone else is talking about?"

Wow, okay. She's upset. She's hurt. She's discouraged. She's scared. She doesn't understand what she's doing wrong. My higher wisdom has a few things to say in response.

"My dear one. I see you are scared and disappointed and tired of waiting for things to go the way you expect. I see you believing that you somehow have a say in this or can control this. There's no such thing as you doing it 'right' or 'wrong.' Do you understand this? You show up each day with your heart wide open, trusting that all that occurs is for you. You remain trusting of that and then move forward. You take action. You feel what you feel. You respond to people. You wake up and do it again. And that's not you doing it 'right'—that's just you being connected to who you truly are and showing up for life. That's you doing exactly what you're here to do. This is also why there is no doing it 'wrong.' It's all just you listening and doing your best to take the next step and then the next and then the next. You can't fail at this. You might like to think that if you read the books and do the meditations and say the prayers and set the intentions and light the sage, you're doing it right and will be worthy and loved. But that's not the case. These things might support you in getting more in touch with the truth that you are already these things. But nothing you do or don't do changes who you truly are. You may feel it at certain times more than others, but that doesn't mean it ever changes or goes away."

"Okay, higher wisdom. Then, what does it mean to be living my 'highest path' and aligned with divine will if I can't do anything wrong or even do anything to change who I already am?"

"Dear child, when you are remembering who you truly are—that you are already worthy and are pure love—you create more experiences in your life that remind you of that on a regular basis. That doesn't mean you won't still fall off your bike from time to time and skin your knees. When things don't go as you think they should, that doesn't mean you're not on your 'highest path.' Maybe more importantly, even if you're 'not on your highest path,' you're still not doing anything wrong. This is the piece you need to hear. Please listen closely. You are not doing anything wrong, no matter what you do. You are inherently good and loved and valuable and worthy just as you are, whether or not you are aligned with what you perceive as your highest path or taking a different route. The deeper you feel this at all times—even, maybe especially when you are faced with what you would otherwise define as a 'failure' or evidence that you didn't do something 'right'—the more you will live into this truth, and it will become a default setting. So, no matter what happens, it won't throw you off or leave you doubting yourself. You will be so grounded in the truth of who you are that it won't matter the external circumstances. You'll have a deeper understanding and appreciation for accepting everything as it is. And that's it: not making it mean anything or define you in any way."

My higher wisdom continued. "It's safe and okay to feel excitement. It's okay to feel the joy of something 'going your way.' Feel the chills, feel the exhilaration and excitement, and remember it doesn't make you any more or less of who you truly are. I believe, in the past, you got your hopes up because you thought, 'Now, I'm loved, worthy, doing it right! Look at what just happened as evidence of that!' Whether that was a boyfriend coming along and promising you something or a job opportunity, a new client, some money, whatever. It's part of the human experience to feel joy and excitement when you meet the guy or get the client or make the money or receive the gift. Just remember that isn't indicative of who you are. That never changes. Even when things change—the guy leaves or stops calling, the client quits, the job doesn't pan out, the bill comes in—that doesn't change who you are either. You aren't being told that you aren't worthy or valued. So, when something doesn't go as you thought it would, it's still all part of your path. It isn't a sign that you're doing something wrong; it is simply what is.

"Accept what is without seeing it as who you are or what you're capable of. Can you feel this? Can you hear this? Getting a new client—it just is. Losing a client just is. Receiving $10,000 just is. Not having $10,000 just is. It's not about what happens externally. You're all these things at your core. No matter what."

I need to hear this wisdom more than I realized I would. These words serve as a balm to my soul. They give me permission to stop shaming myself and questioning everything I do. While writing about my journey to becoming enough, I am revealing that I have the belief that receiving from others is an indication of my lacking something. This is interesting. I realize how I attach the belief of receiving from others to prove my long-held belief that I'm not enough as I am. If I have to depend on others, this is proof that I am not capable of doing it on my own, that I haven't tried hard enough—that same familiar story. I've lived with this broken record for nearly thirty-five years.

The publisher reaches out again to see if I've made a decision. When I speak with her, I tell her how much I would love to hire her but can't afford to. She holds space to brainstorm with me the various ways I might attract the necessary resources. After a few days of contemplation, I decide to launch an all-or-nothing crowdfunding campaign to raise the amount I need to publish my book.

Feeling encouraged, I join a friend for yoga in the park the next morning, where I receive a vision. I hear the words "Awaken Village." Village? Like some kind of community? I mean, I suppose being supported by my parents and now asking for support from others is offering me a glimpse into what it means to be a part of a village. I see how interconnected we all are and the power of coming together with a shared vision or intention. I'm not well-versed in intentional communities, but it is the first thought that comes to mind. Am I to create something like that? I don't even know what they are or how they work. Another idea I have is some sort of recovery center, which I also don't know how to create. But what does make sense to me is that we are not meant to do life alone—we are interdependent beings and stronger together. Much like what Ayahuasca showed me, Michael's dis-ease is not his alone. He is not the only one struggling. We all have something to recover—our true selves.

Between living with my parents and embarking on a crowdfunding campaign, I am getting plenty of opportunities to explore my relation-ship with my true self, along with receiving and surrendering control. Asking my parents, who love me unconditionally, for support was one thing. Reaching out to friends, acquaintances, and even strangers, though, brings up a lot. I find myself asking some familiar questions. Am I worthy? Am I deserving? Am I pushing too hard? Am I not doing enough? How do I surrender to the outcome and still do my part?

With the launch of my crowdfunding campaign, I have to look these questions and some initial shame square in the eye. Why is it I don't believe I am deserving of receiving what I desire? Because I continue to hear the fear-based voice within saying that who I am is not inherently good or worthy. I thought I had already learned these lessons, stepping more fully into asking for help when I moved back home. Just as with life, there is always a deeper layer to reveal. A deeper layer to explore. Now, I realize I still have a belief that asking for this money means I am being lazy. I mean, who am I to do what I want and have others pay for it? Other people work hard to have what they want; why do I think I can just ask and it will be given?

Is this why I (and so many others) have a hard time receiving? Do we have this conscious or unconscious belief that there is something lacking, and (even though that isn't true) we don't want to acknowledge it? And that we, therefore, block our ability to receive from others as a way to prove to ourselves (and others) that we are already whole and complete? If I believe the reason I don't have money at times is because I'm not smart enough or capable enough to earn more of it, then receiving money from another person may very well feel like proof that I am indeed *not* smart or capable enough to do it on my own. See how that works?

As I am writing about in my book, that's just another shield. It's another way of keeping out what we already have within. And unfortunately, it has the opposite effect from what we desire and perpetuates our false beliefs. When we allow ourselves to receive, it might at first feel like we are lacking, which can feel uncomfortable. But, ultimately, we begin learning how this isn't true. In truth, it isn't because we're broken or lacking something within that we ask to receive something. It is by openly receiving that we are reminded of all that we already are because what is within is reflected back to us from without.

This is evident in the way I'm being supported by my parents and those contributing to my campaign. This is the shift in perspective: what I receive is a reflection of my inner thoughts and beliefs. Because I'm finally ready to receive from this place of wholeness, I'm attracting people into my life who want to give to me. And as I receive, doing so becomes easier and more satisfying. I am able to enjoy receiving from my crowdfunding supporters and from my parents as I stay at their house and eat their food, realizing that my "neediness" is not an indication that I'm inadequate or doing anything wrong. Rather, I am complete and whole, and I *also* need things from others.

Still, it is tempting to slip into old thought patterns and forget this truth, but that is a natural part of the process. At times, I find myself worrying that I won't be able to provide for myself again in the future, as if I've lost that ability. I still need to remind myself that, even though I am able to receive from others, I am also capable of taking care of myself. And I know that life will be full of opportunities to remind me of this.

This process helps me get clearer on what I want to experience in all areas of my life. I don't want or need to be taken care of because I am incapable or somehow lacking in and of myself. I want to experience the pleasure of receiving from a place of wholeness and give back in return. As I am learning from *A Course in Miracles*, a channeled book I have been reading and meditating on daily, to give is to receive, and to receive is to give. They are interchangeable. To receive is also a way of reflecting back to others their own wholeness as we validate ours. It is a way of giving back to the person who is giving. Therefore, when we receive from another, we are giving a gift to them. With my crowdfunding campaign, what I receive through this campaign is given back to the giver as a reflection of their generous and abundant nature.

There is a pattern, though, that keeps coming up along this journey: I clearly ask for what I want, thinking that I'm stepping out and acting courageously in doing so, and then it doesn't turn out how I want. When I first launched my campaign a few weeks ago, I thought the only work I had to do was release my shame, be vulnerable, and ask for what I need. Then, people would do what I asked in the way I thought they would. I (unconsciously) thought I got to control other people's actions. Guess what? I don't. Some people eagerly give a small amount. Some give generously. Some ignore the request. Some are triggered by it. A few actually say they won't support me because I need to earn this myself.

Just because I ask to receive does not mean I will, especially in the way I think or expect. There is a lesson even in that. Both in being content with the "no" (and not making it mean anything about me) as well as "things might not always turn out the way I want" because I may not consciously know the bigger picture. I am being invited to remember that I am still worthy and valued and loved in the face of these "failures." I can deepen into my trust that all is working for me, even when I can't yet see how. I am being asked to trust that this is a co-creative effort and part of a larger plan.

In the final days of my crowdfunding campaign, I'm not sure I'll reach my goal as I'm still short a couple thousand dollars. Not because I don't believe in myself or think I'm deserving but simply because I accept this as a possibility. It isn't a mindset of defeat; it is one of acceptance. I've made it quite clear what I desire to create and how others can support me. I've asked for what I want. Now, it's time to pull in my anchor, get back to creating what I'm here to create, and surrender all the rest.

My book didn't start when I launched my crowdfunding campaign. It started long before that—with an idea, an inkling, an inspiration. This is how all things start. Like a seed that's planted and takes years of being watered and receiving sunlight to blossom into the thing it is today. And, just like nature, it takes less doing and more being on my part than I might think. It's not that I don't do anything—but the practice is to get out of the way more than it is to make it happen.

Surrender means ceasing resistance and completely submitting. As much as I talk about "the universe," I'm not always willing to fully submit to it. This is what is being asked of me at this point in my journey. I have attempted to do it my way for quite some time now. I believe this is one of those things I have done to protect myself, and that no longer serves me. This is where trust and faith come into play, even when it isn't easy. I have been gaining trust in myself; now I get to trust the universe.

On November 11, the final day of my campaign, I receive the message that my goal is reached. Tears fill my eyes. We did it! This hasn't been just about reaching a goal. It has proven that it takes a village to bring anything into existence. I couldn't have done this all by myself, and I didn't. It feels clearer than ever: we aren't meant to do life alone.

I am reminded that reaching a goal is not a means to an end but rather something I can fully engage in each and every step of the way, no matter the final outcome. I notice a rush of excitement as I now shift focus away from this campaign to the creation and publishing of my book. I am confident that I am an even clearer channel now, ready to bring this message into the world because of this experience.

I anchor to a new belief—I am no better or worse than anyone else. It is not because I'm worse than someone else that I suffer at times, and it is not because I am better or at a "higher vibration" that I experience joy and bliss. It all just is, and whatever is meant to happen will happen.

As the leaves fall to the ground, I am reminded that by allowing our false beliefs to fall away, we reveal our true nature. Many of us fear we will no longer exist without them. Just look at the trees to remember how that is not the case. The tree is still a tree even after it loses its leaves. It will even sprout new leaves in spring. So, too, with us. But first, some part of it must die before it can be reborn. It must be non-attached to the current leaves it has, surrendering to the season it finds itself in and standing naked, which is a very vulnerable thing to do. Now, it is time for me to release the beliefs that have offered me protection and shade all these years and see what new growth will come.

CHAPTER 5

WASTING TIME

With the smell of coffee wafting through the air and spring showers falling from the sky, the words "vulnerability" and "submission" come up during another one of my regular chats with Clint. We discuss the importance and helpfulness of cocooning—how it is essential and necessary for the healing process and the preparation for a new life. He sees how I have created a very small world for myself after moving into my parents' house—one that I can pretty easily control—so that I can heal, repair, and prepare. I have some inkling, but I'm not entirely sure what exactly I'm preparing for. I know things are changing and will need to change even more. By now, my intended three-month reset has turned into more than a year. I'm so ready to move on, but I still have some hesitation.

This cocoon has offered me lots of time to remember who I am (and complete my book about it as well as record nearly one hundred podcast episodes to share these revelations with the world). As I say at the end of my book, "Once you step out of judgment, you have the opportunity to accept everything as it is so that you can then surrender to the journey, which brings with it a whole other slew of enemies, allies, and treasures—processing shame, learning to live in the both/and, finding your balance. Once you recognize your enough-ness and gain the treasure of becoming the Observer—trusting your innate perfection, knowing, and connection—a whole new layer of the onion awaits. This becoming is the beginning, not the end." It is becoming clear that accepting and surrendering to the journey is the next layer for me to explore.

For many years now, I feel all I've been doing is surrendering, but it seems I am being asked to do even more. While in my cocoon, more layers of who I have thought I am have been stripped away from me, revealing the exposed skin underneath. My friend mentions how it can feel vulnerable when we've been hurt in the past and carry a memory of that hurt with us into new situations. My leaps of faith have resulted in some very uncomfortable and even painful experiences, and my discomfort with vulnerability means I am fearful of full surrender. Unfamiliar territory pokes my tender spots, pointing me back to where I might still be afraid of feeling pain and experiencing past wounds as they heal. In typical Clint style, he connects my personal experience of life to something bigger. After a recent bike accident that left him with a broken clavicle, he tells me how the healing process is actually more painful than the initial injury. Pain doesn't mean healing isn't occurring; it often means it is.

For the past year, I have been gaining greater clarity about my sore spots and, specifically, my relationship patterns. For as long as I can remember, I have had a tendency to attract unavailable men (and other scenarios). It started when I was a teenager and fell in love with two separate boys (one of whom I lost my virginity to). Both of them came out of the closet after high school.

Since then, I have continued to go through life attracted to men who, for one reason or another, aren't able to give me what I want. Something deep within me knows I was drawn to them for a reason, but I don't know what it is. Am I here to free them? I think about my partnership with Michael. I have wanted so desperately to love him free from his addiction. I have felt in my bones that if I could just love him enough, he would experience greater freedom. I have felt that I could love him enough for him to get sober. I could love him enough for him to become available. I could love him enough for him to love me the way I desire. I could want it badly enough and hold the vision long enough for me to get it. I see how this pattern has kept me stuck.

In this cocoon, I have come to some powerful revelations about why Michael and I were brought together. Michael has been one of my greatest mentors in unconditional love, both toward myself and others. He has helped me learn to love and let go. Ram Dass talks about how a guru isn't someone who has all the answers or knowledge—a guru is a mirror, someone who reflects back to us who we are by shining a light on the dark places as well as reflecting our light back to us. Michael is my "gu" (dark) and "ru" (light). He is the first paradox I have consciously experienced, but neither of us is ready to hold the tension of both opposites simultaneously. We aren't experiencing pure oneness or unity because we operate from codependency, enabling each of us to perpetuate unhealthy behaviors and beliefs.

On multiple occasions, this manifests in the thoughts I have after yelling at Michael for drinking too much. I find myself thinking, "I don't know what's wrong with me. I don't want to be unloving or unkind. I want to be gentle, but I don't know if I know how. I want to fully accept that this is his way of being in the world. Why can't I do that? Am I supposed to? Why can't I love him as unconditionally as he loves me?" I go to bed noticing a lot of anger and frustration and resistance in my body. I am still holding on in this push-and-pull cycle with both Michael and the lessons I am learning. I interpret the contractions I am experiencing as a sign that there is growth about to happen, that I'm preparing to expand and grow into a person who can love and accept Michael just as he is.

The move to Sioux Falls hasn't been easy for me, and it really hasn't been for him, living in a city where he doesn't know anyone else and is without a steady income or resources to fall back on. And understand-ably so. It's hard enough for me to live with my family again, and they're my flesh and blood. Michael's drinking has gotten even worse by now, resulting in some unsettling episodes—totaling my car, getting a third DUI, having to take a breathalyzer test twice a day at the county jail (which I drive him to), sometimes not passing and ending up in jail for a day (or longer), losing various jobs, and, eventually, being homeless after finally being asked to leave my parents' house a few months ago. I must say, dating a man who takes me on a date to the soup kitchen is fraught with challenges and isn't quite what I had in mind when it comes to my life partner and being provided for. Still, I love him, enable him, and don't let go.

I continue navigating the layers of attachment, pain, and growth that have come with this relationship. It takes a toll on me. After being with Michael for nearly four years, I often find myself deeply sad and depressed, like I want to curl into a ball and cry or scream. It isn't easy loving someone who has so deeply forgotten who he is. He has such a pure soul. I saw and felt it straightaway. It is hard to watch him cover that up, numb that, dim that light, so to speak. I see him as this incredibly gentle, loving, compassionate man who simply can't give those things to himself. He loves me unconditionally but can't love himself that way. He isn't able to see the capable man I see underneath the surface.

I feel for the part of me who still doesn't see what's going on (with tremendous compassion because we can't see even the obvious until we are ready to see). Even if this part of me has friends and loved ones who can see it clear as day and have said as much and some part of her deep within knows they might be right, she isn't ready to see it herself. She has been so unclear on how to make sense of this relationship. She has accepted such poor behavior and treatment from her partner because she loves him, yet she is still learning to love herself uncon- ditionally. She still isn't fully accepting of all that she is, including the parts that are fed up. She hasn't yet freed herself enough to accept what she wants and is willing to put up with.

One morning, I awake reflecting on the night before. I had found out Michael is drinking again after his stint in rehab. I am so hurt, I feel as if my heart is literally breaking. It's not even about the drinking, even though his relationship with alcohol is very dysfunctional. If it were, I'd feel that way anytime anybody drinks (myself included). It's what I'm making it mean. That I'm not enough. Not enough to keep him from drinking. Not worth changing for. I realize I have internalized this issue, personalized it and made it all about me.

I send Michael a message saying, "I was so angry last night because I was afraid. Afraid I am wrong. Wrong about you, wrong about us. But that's not possible. It's not about right and wrong. It's not about others saying, 'I told you so.' It's about trusting myself at all times. I can still love you. Your behavior has nothing to do with me." Saying this feels so freeing. Like a weight off my shoulders. I don't have to carry the burden of his actions or stay stuck in my head about what they mean.

My tendency is to feel like I'm wrong and then want to prove others wrong in defense. What all of this is really teaching me is that I can trust my own experience and opinions. I can trust how I feel and what I think is true (at least in the moment). It doesn't matter what others think or whether or not they agree with me. This is my experience and my journey. There's no need to defend or prove it. There's only this moment and trusting what I feel, think, and experience. It doesn't mean that's "better" than someone else's experience; it's simply best for *me* (and what's "best" might even change).

What is it my soul desires? What is it I am here to evolve? What is my path? What I'm beginning to realize more fully is that there are infinite paths and, therefore, infinite perspectives. That's what makes life so beautiful and dynamic. We each get to choose what resonates, supports, and serves us in each moment. I can hear the opinions and desires of others without the need to justify myself or resent them. I can remain true to what is true for me.

Can I stand in my own power and avoid taking Michael's journey personally? Can I allow him to have his experience even if I don't think his choices are "best" for him and know they're not best for me? I love Michael and believe that he is pure love. We all, in fact, are love. We are all divine. His soul, too, is on its journey, and his journey is his own. I don't get to control it, and I don't need to stick my nose in it. I can still choose to love him. So long as I don't give into my victimhood or lie to myself or give into Michael's fears or victimhood or lies to himself. I can stand in love, truth, honesty, trust, and responsibility. That's the "best" I can do.

One day, as if on cue, I receive two very similar messages from two very different sources. I am doing my morning reading of *A Course in Miracles*, and the lesson is "Let me be still and listen to truth today." Afterward, I go to church with my parents, where the pastor talks about the importance of "wasting time" by slowing down and listening (to God and to others). He points out that it is in the slowing down, the "wasting" of time, that real transformation occurs. He points out the importance of being with others, especially when there's nothing we can do to change them, like in a nursing home or in hospice (or, I think to myself, in addiction). We so often wish to see results from our actions, to know we are making a difference or "being of service," yet when working with the elderly or infirmed, there isn't much we can do. All we can do is accept that they are still going to die.

The next day, facing a highly intoxicated Michael yet again, these mantras and teachings float around my awareness. There always seems to be a part of me that wants to be mad and confront, but I try something new. I stop working on what I had been thinking was so important to accomplish. Instead, I just sit with him. I listen to his ramblings. I watch him get upset. I witness his mental illness in full bloom. I gaze into his eyes as much as I can. I say nothing. I don't ask questions. I don't try to fix him.

I notice my discomfort is still there, telling me, "He's getting too loud," or "He might break that." A few times, I even step in and say "no" when he attempts to throw something. But for the most part, I just listen. I recite my own lessons in my head. I listen for truth and only truth, and I am finally able to see his dis-ease for what it is. I recognize him as somebody I can't change. It feels like a huge relief. Like I can finally exhale. As I do so, I am fascinated by the response. Soon enough, he calms down. With nothing to fight against aside from himself, he stops. It seems we have both stopped fighting. Our white flags are waving. We have surrendered.

Throughout this relationship, I have had a constant thought: Am I spending too much time on this person and his issues? Am I spending enough time on my own? I mean, I have a mission here on this planet—I have books to write, podcast episodes to record, a village to co-create. And immediately, I recall the voice of the pastor: "We need to spend more time and more love on others, especially when it seems to be a waste. It is in turning away from self-preference, self-promotion, and self-preservation and toward reckless love that we gain our life." So, this is my duty. I am called to "waste my life" on another who is in greater need than me, even if I have a hard time accepting it. I experience a deeper understanding and integration of what it truly means to surrender, as vulnerable as that is. I let it and him be.

How often do we take time just to listen and be with others without our own agendas in mind? How often do we do that when they are acting in ways that seem inappropriate or unacceptable? How often do we let others, and ourselves, just be? I am finally seeing the value of doing just this. I feel myself beginning to embody what it means to let go.

The thing is, even when I am willing to accept the unacceptable nature of Michael's relationship with alcohol, I continue to resist what is to me the most unacceptable thing: that life, no matter what, sometimes hurts and that there's nothing I can do about it. Things will end. Change will happen. People will die. Things happen that don't make sense. Nothing lasts. There's nothing I can do "enough" to stop that or prevent that from happening.

I am afraid to accept my life as it is and myself as I am because I find them unacceptable. The money I have (or don't have), the sadness and anger I feel, the weight I gain, the mistakes I make, the defeats I encounter—I resist all of it. Because life isn't *supposed* to be painful. People aren't supposed to hurt me, and I'm not supposed to hurt them. I'm not supposed to fail.

I'm also afraid of claiming what I want out of fear that I'll lose it. In order to get out of my own way, I have to let go of everything standing in my way. And what if I am the only thing standing in my way? I have to let go of these beliefs once and for all. I have to be willing to fail and be disappointed. I have to be willing to choose and declare and put a stake in the ground. I have to be willing to not know how any of this works or how anything will unfold. I have to be willing to, once again, step into the unknown.

We are so afraid of accepting what is because we are afraid of accepting who we are. We do not accept ourselves (or God or others) because we believe we are inherently bad and, therefore, undeserving of acceptance, love, and connection. As Paul Tillich says in *The Courage to Be*, we see ourselves as unlovely or unlovable and, therefore, "sin," or, as he defines it, separate ourselves from ourselves, others, and God. "Grace," on the other hand, is acceptance—accepting what we see as unacceptable, namely the self—and deep down, we do not believe we are worthy of this. This is the ultimate conundrum, the ultimate fear.

In addition to receiving support through books and sermons, I am invited to attend a breathwork session with my friend. It is a very powerful practice to regulate the nervous system, release what no longer serves you, and experience expanded states of consciousness. The following Sunday, I join a few other people at my yoga studio, where we are guided through a kundalini breathwork sequence. As I lie on my mat, listening to the music and finding the rhythm of the ongoing in-in-out breath, I start to go deep within myself.

What will my life look like if I continue to accept the unacceptable? How in the world do I dare do that? "We accept the acceptance of the unacceptable," Tillich's words play in my ears. Instead of resisting what is as "not okay," we accept it as part of the bigger picture. Ultimately, when we refuse to accept the unacceptable, we remain in resistance to death. Eventually, everything dies—when we accept this, just as when we observe it, we transform its very nature. Acceptance shifts our experience of these difficult events. These events still happen, but they no longer seem inherently evil. When we accept what is, we are living in alignment with the reality of the moment. We are honoring the present and seeing things for how they truly are, not how we wish they were. I can feel that this initial accepting is the beginning of the end of my struggle.

Acceptance isn't pretending everything is okay. Acceptance is being with exactly what is as it is—disappointment, excitement, desire, wishing

I could connect more and not being able to, or what have you—and being honest about that with myself and possibly with others. But it is vulnerable to surrender control. In order to let go, we must first feel safe. Riding an unsteady bike, you'll hold tighter to the handlebars. If you feel confident and secure, it can even feel fun to let go. Freedom feels more accessible when we feel secure. In this way, true freedom is rooted in security.

During the session, my facilitator uses another anchor analogy. This time, I see a hot air balloon wanting to take off. Tears fill my eyes once again. My body gets chills. Now that I have detached from some of my beliefs anchoring me down, this intense emotion confirms that Michael is still my anchor. I don't blame him; he's simply a reflection of my own inner anchors, and by staying attached to him, I have perpetuated my own beliefs and limitations.

I have been holding onto him for dear life, avoiding freeing myself from my own limitations. Finally, after my years of resisting, I find myself ready to let go of the man I love. It's taken me slowing down, feeling the security of living with my parents, and giving myself (and him) permission to just be. The moment has come. It is time to cut the line and soar.

When I return home, I call Michael and we both agree we need to let each other go. I give myself some time and space to be with this ending. Then, I feel aware of another anchor. The cocoon of my parents' home is beginning to confine me. It has provided the external safety and security I have needed to develop these feelings internally. As I develop greater self-acceptance, I am ready to more confidently and securely make decisions and take the next step. The healing has occurred, and the cast has become a hindrance, keeping me from the movement and expansion I desire and know await me. It's time to spread my wings and fly, trusting that the wind will carry me. Yet I'm still scared of the uncertainty of what is next.

Reflecting on my life, I see how I've always valued freedom. The "problem" is that I have believed that making decisions and commitments necessarily limits freedom. The security of being tied to something has felt like the opposite of being free. Being free to make spontaneous choices has been my safe zone, though it has often disguised underlying fear. While I see the necessity of cutting myself free from Michael, I see there is nothing wrong with safety and security coming in other forms. What we define as security, and whether that security is rooted in fear, is what determines whether we're limited. Security can free us or imprison us; it's our choice.

There is an interesting relationship between security and freedom. For many, weighing every option, comparing pros and cons, and making decisions based on what's "right" creates a feeling of certainty. It is the comfort of this false security (because let's be honest: nothing is absolutely secure, and everything is at risk of falling away at any moment) that creates the belief that we are free to do the next thing.

This is where the illusion is found. We get the word "secure" from the Latin "securus," meaning "free from care." Oxford defines it as "the state of feeling safe, stable, and free from fear or anxiety." Security is something *within*, not something that is given to us or created outside of us. It isn't a structure or an object or a thing we can point to. It is a personal experience based on a feeling, not a reality or an actuality. It is not "the state of *being* safe, stable, and free from fear or anxiety."

Beneath the security this home has offered me, I find the next layer of perceived insecurity: the belief that I also need the security of clarity before *being* free to leave. I have used clarity as a safety net. I believe I needed to know *how* things would happen before doing them. Many of us use getting clear on something to give us the security we need to take the next step. So long as I believed I had clarity, I have felt more secure.

It makes sense: if I can clearly see the path in front of me, I can more confidently take the next step, assured that I won't step on something dangerous or step in a puddle or walk right off the edge of a cliff. (Of course, that assumes there won't be a net to catch me.) What if I don't get to have this? Is it even possible to know? Is this one of those unacceptable things that we must accept about the human experience? What will happen if I try living in a space of complete unknowing?

Just like when I feel sick (or need to purge during an Ayahuasca journey), the best thing I can do is surrender, let myself feel the discomfort for a short amount of time, and then release it. This discomfort is my body's way of letting me know it's healing. It is time to let go and fully surrender to the process, not knowing what's to come. Simply observe, accept, release. Observe the questions. Observe the sensations. Observe the beliefs. Observe it all. Notice what is happening, accept what is, and release all need to control or understand.

I may not be able to know the future, but I do have an inner knowing. This is one of the paradoxes of life—simultaneously embracing uncertainty and knowing. I see that there is a balance between "total clarity" and "total blindness." Clarity is essential. Clarity is who we are. Equally, it can serve as an excuse, a delay, a distraction. It can be the mind's way of ignoring the knowing within. My inner knowing, which I tapped into during my Ayahuasca journeys, is telling me everything is going to be okay, that there is a larger plan and everything is an opportunity to raise my consciousness. I may not be clear on when I will attract more clients, how many books I will sell, if I will become a bestselling author, how I will afford living on my own, how I will find a place to live with no stable income, but I know I am always supported. I know I am safe to follow my heart's desires. This is true security.

Without inner security, we can get stuck in the incessant, endless search for clarity. We can be unwilling to trust the soft, subtle inner voice, which already knows what our soul desires. We wait and wait and wait for more certainty, but there is no need to wait before taking the next step. Like when our eyes adjust to a dark room and we begin to see more and more of what's in front of us, clarity reveals itself to us. Get quiet—listen for the clarity that is already within. And then surrender, and surrender some more. We don't need further clarity on *how* things will unfold; we need greater willingness to follow the path of clarity as it unfolds, as if by magic.

CHAPTER 6

TRUSTING THE FLOW

"What do you *want?*" Sitting on a bench in the park near my parents' house with the sun on my face, enjoying the hot August air, I'm on the phone with a very close friend who is supporting me through the desire to find my own place despite not knowing how I'll afford it. She suggests I get crystal clear on what I want. After my recent thoughts about how clarity can feel like a hindrance, this feels counterintuitive. As I keep listening, though, I realize she's not asking me to get clear on how this will happen but rather on what I desire.

"Describe the perfect apartment," she tells me. "Write it down." It's one of the first times in my life that I get to consciously choose where I want to live. I am no longer using clarity as an excuse nor feeling afraid to get clear on what I want for fear I won't get it or be disappointed, so I make a list of what that is. Lots of natural light. High ceilings. Bright space with white walls. Close enough to walk downtown without needing a car. Hardwood floors. Bathtub. It's not a long list, but it's all I need.

Within a few days, I'm looking at an apartment with all of these qualities. The day I sign the lease, I am offered a freelance writing job that pays the exact rent price every month on retainer for the next three months. As it has before, the path becomes clear as soon as I act on my desires and follow my soul's impulse. These are the signs and reminders I need in order to know I am safe. I can take the leap, and

I will be supported. There is nothing wrong with moving on. I don't need to wait for the "right" time. I simply have to act.

The year-long lease now locked in, I feel happy. Within weeks, I get my first "book doula" client, who has hired me to help edit and publish her book under my imprint, Awaken Village Press, the current iteration of my vision. After I realized I wasn't in any place (and might not be for a while) to create a physical village, the original inspiration shifted into an idea for a publishing company to awaken the planet one book at a time. With one book under my belt and many experiences coaching others (along with a little encouragement from Clint), it felt like a natural merging of my gifts to guide others through the process of writing and birthing their books. With the money she pays me, I am able to hire the designer who creates the logo I place on her book and many more to come. I soon attract three more clients to go on the journey of writing and publishing their books. I feel like I'm finding my flow.

These newfound elements of security falling into place don't mean losing my free-spirited and open-hearted style. Within weeks, I meet Eric, a guy who's temporarily in town for work, and get the wild urge to leave all this behind and follow him out west where he lives. Exploring life with Eric, just as free-spirited as me, sounds adventurous and exciting.

But wait ... I just signed a lease, and now I want to leave? Am I afraid of commitment? In some ways, I know I am. But something deeper is also going on. My heart isn't in Sioux Falls. It is providing me with a temporary home. This I have known for more than two years. I want to find my *home* home. And, since I can literally live anywhere in the world, I have figured I'll find my home when I meet my person. So, what if this is him? Well, I'm certainly willing to find out! I know I want the freedom to go wherever I want, whenever I want. But, even with that knowing, I am once again afraid of being impulsive and choosing wrong. I mean, I just met this guy. What if it doesn't work out? Am I being impatient? Should I wait for a "better time" to give my notice? Should I wait for when I have more money first? Am I trying to force things?

Two months after moving into my apartment, I'm on the phone again with my friend, who responds to my concerns with this wisdom:

"There is no such thing as doing the wrong thing. If you choose to stay in Sioux Falls, in your apartment, with your five jobs,"—yes, a girl's gotta do what a girl's gotta do—"does that feel like being true to yourself?"

I resound with a definitive, clear NO. This is the one thing I don't ever waver on or feel ungrounded about. Being true to myself means following my soul's desires and impulses, even when they seem completely irrational. So, I give my notice and ask if I can get out of my lease as soon as they find someone to take over, knowing it won't take them long to rent out this unit again.

By the time all this happens, within a matter of weeks, the thing with Eric is over. Still, I am determined to stay true to myself and leave. I give my thirty-day notice. But what does that mean, knowing my heart isn't here? Where to this time? I've learned that part of my human design is a sacral authority. I respond to life from my gut, which means I need something that I can respond to with a yes or no. When posed with a question like, "Where do I want to live?" I freeze. According to the woman who gave me my human design reading back in 2015, I don't have access to my desires when presented this way. So, instead, I will let the universe show me where I am to go next.

At times, I interpret my need for the universe to guide me as evidence that I am still afraid to choose or unclear about what I truly want. I believe the universe chooses for me, and I simply go with the flow. But what I am struggling to grasp is whether responding to what is put on my path *is* choosing.

When I am notified that a new tenant has been found for my unit and I am free to move out on the first of the month, it feels like everything is falling into place. The only thing missing is the small detail of where I am moving to. Once more, with no Plan B, I share my decision to leave on social media and organize a "Ciao for Now" party to say goodbye. I invite a few friends over to commemorate this place I have called home and this group of people I have gotten to know over the past few years. We stand around drinking wine and eating snacks in my bright kitchen, reminiscing on good times and how much has changed for me since moving to Sioux Falls. The sounds of talking and laughing bounce off the hardwood floors and high ceilings. Then, the question of what I'm doing next comes up. I get perplexed looks and questions about my decision to leave an amazing apartment without any idea where I'm going. Crazy, right? But I am learning to embrace that this is who I am! This is me freeing myself from anything that keeps me from being more of me. This is me living authentically and bravely and boldly and willingly and fearlessly and fully and faithfully. And isn't my whole mission here to be good with being me? To be *more* of me?

For most of my life, I have resisted and questioned who I am. I have believed I might find a different way of experiencing *my* life. Standing amongst my friends, celebrating this new chapter, I no longer want to run away from me. I no longer want to pretend I'm somebody else. I no longer want to apologize for who I am in my essence. I no longer want to look for how I "should" do it differently. I'm not suggesting that other people's essence needs to look like mine. A bunch of people all running around, picking up and leaving whenever inspiration strikes, moving from one thing to another, leaving a trail of love and pain and confusion and bliss in their wake—that would be a nightmare! I don't expect anyone to understand why I do what I do. Heck, I don't often understand it. I'm *finally* starting to see that's the whole point. I simply hear the call from deep within and am learning to listen and follow without any further answers or explanations or rationalizations. This is enough. This is who I am. And I desire to be the fullest expression of *me* that I can be.

In order to support this, I am guided to schedule an appointment with a psychic. A friend had told me about her session with this woman, and I immediately knew I was to schedule one for myself for November 11 (another 11/11). I've only had one reading with a psychic years earlier when I first left my corporate job, and I have no expectations other than being open and ready to receive.

The morning of the phone appointment, she opens with a prayer before spending forty-five minutes or so on my energy field and what my guides have to say. She mentions my playfulness, my power, my free spirit, how I show up in relationships, how I love without abandon, and my story that I'm not enough and unwanted (but am actually adored). It's time, she says, to let that story go. She hesitates before straightforwardly saying that I'm going to be in love and have a baby. This brings tears to my eyes.

Before our session ends, I ask a question. I mention that I am moving out of my apartment on December 1 and have been praying every day for a sign of where I'm meant to go next. "Is there a chance your landlord would let you stay?" she asks. I am caught off guard, explaining that someone has already signed a lease on my apartment. "You might want to ask if there's another unit available. I'm not telling you what to do; you have to follow your gut. But you're not done here yet. It feels nurturing and like 'home.' It's okay to stay in Sioux Falls for a while."

I start to cry even harder. I am exhausted by being wishy-washy and constantly second-guessing myself. She assures me that she understands and says, "A bigger word is coming in: trusting. For some reason, I feel you don't trust. That if you aren't in action or in the driver's seat or in control, the universe won't give you what you want. That if you're not the one doing it, it's not going to happen. Don't be in a hurry. You get to relax." Hearing her say that summons my feeling of security.

During my meeting with her, I learn that according to my guides, my first action to take is trusting I'm okay. That love is coming, partnership is coming, a child is coming, success is here. Trust that if I bring my gifts and joy into the world, then everything is going to fall into place. "Ask your landlord if another unit is available," she tells me. "Have a solid home base you can use as your anchor." I start to wonder if an anchor isn't always a bad thing. Maybe it doesn't just hold us back; it can also secure us.

Even though it seems highly unlikely another unit will be available, I contact my property owner as soon as we hang up the phone. Setting aside my embarrassment for having just given my notice, I ask if there happen to be any others I could move into. She quickly responds, "Actually, unit one is vacating by the end of the month. I have a showing for it this afternoon. Unless you want it." Sight unseen, I say yes. Within a few weeks, I transfer my lease and move my belongings to the unit downstairs. It is smaller, but I realize that my overwhelming feeling is gratitude for how everything works out.

And then a shame bubble creeps up for having recently told everyone I was leaving just to stay in the same building. But it also occurs to me that I am free to change my mind, even on a dime. I've been so afraid of making the "wrong" choices that I instead waver between choices, causing distress in the long run because I'm not clear with myself, others, or the universe. We often see changing our minds as a sign of weakness or lack of integrity, but I'm starting to see how it can be a sign of being fully present to what is in each and every moment and responding to that. It's having the courage to speak one's truth despite what others might think. It's following our hearts. At times, it is a sign of humility because it puts on vulnerable display our deepest, unfiltered desires along with any potential guilt or shame.

It seems that we as humans don't like to change our minds because change indicates groundlessness. It means we don't know the future, which creates stress and anxiety. People who change their minds (or change themselves) are people we feel we can't predict, which feels unsafe. It all stems from our desire for constancy and assuredness. The thing is, nothing in the physical realm is constant. Our need to make decisions and stick with them is an erroneous way of attempting to find solidity where none exists.

As I swap out one lease for another, I reflect on commitment. Commitment is often our way of offering ourselves and others a sense of assuredness. We commit to something in the hopes that doing so will offer us security, and in a way, it does. We get married and feel more secure knowing we have a person to love and be loved by. We buy a house and feel more secure knowing we have a place to live. And there's nothing wrong with desiring security. But we often forget that everything changes. And the fact that nothing is permanent doesn't need to prevent us from committing.

Some of us resist changing our minds because we believe it means we are breaking a commitment, even though it may simply mean a new commitment is being made. Commitment means being dedicated to something, pledging to do or undertake something. This can only ever be done in a given moment. It doesn't have to mean "forever and ever, amen." I can be dedicated to something for a minute or for fifty years. I can pledge to do something now and then undertake something else in the future (which is just another now). There is great honor in keeping one's word and upholding one's commitment. But when it is done from a place of fear or control, that's a different story. If the only reason I don't change my mind (or let you change yours) is because I'm afraid of what might happen or what others might think, then I've trapped myself (or you). This is when the need for false security becomes a prison.

For many of us, once a decision is made, we feel more in control, no longer in limbo, leaving it up to chance. Again, there's nothing wrong with that. We control things so we can know them. The fear of not knowing drives most of our actions as humans. Not knowing if our lover will stay or go. Not knowing if we will be promoted or terminated. Not knowing if we will meet our future partner. Not knowing if we will get the client. Not knowing if we will have a lot of money. Not knowing when our life will end. We make plans so we can know what to expect. We pass judgments on people and hold grudges and create boundaries so we can be "sure" whatever has happened doesn't happen again. We try to control all of it. Through commitment, through manifestation, through prayer, through all sorts of means.

Control is a way to create the illusion of security. Yet being secure is feeling free from care and, therefore, free from the need for control. Interesting how they are indeed one and the same—security and freedom. If we desire to feel secure (safe, stable, free from anxiety), it starts with releasing any insecurity we have about ourselves (all those places we still overly care about), which occurs as we accept all parts of ourselves. So, here's the paradox: the more secure we feel, the more free we can be.

Instead of focusing on how to control our environment or those around us to make us feel secure (which we know isn't a real thing anyway—because the ultimate truth is that nothing lasts forever), why not focus on cultivating that feeling of security within? Why not focus on accepting who we truly are—and this isn't only in reference to some godly, idealized form but also to the human form, rooted in deep self-acceptance of what is? This is where true security is found. After all, if I can't trust myself to be secure—if I don't feel secure in my body and who I am—how can I ever trust what's outside of me? I guess this is what I could now spend my time and energy on—accepting who I truly am and living from that place of security, from that state of being free from danger or threat. I start to experience so much less anxiety when I simply make a choice about something and reduce the decision time. As I remember who I truly am, what is there to fear?

Walking back in the cold to my new apartment after a lovely Christmas lunch with my friend Clint, this revelation hits me like a ton of bricks. It dawns on me that, were I to die in this moment, I would be at peace with that. The thought itself makes me a bit uncomfortable, and yet there is this soothing acceptance along with it. I recognize in this moment that I have loved; offered my gifts; been of service; lived an honest, bold, and brave life; and experienced many wonderful things. What more could a person hope for? Isn't that what life is all about?

In this recognition comes great peace. There is no more I need to "strive" for. There is less I need to fear or attempt to control. There are still things I would love to experience and accomplish in my life—yet, overall, I'm content in this moment. It's an unusual feeling, I'll admit. And, for the first time, it's not as scary a thought as it has been in the past. In the past, it was as if being content with death meant getting hit by a bus any minute now. And I suppose that might happen—I'm not ultimately in control. But I'm no longer afraid of being at peace with death. Did you catch that? Not just no longer fearing death itself, but no longer fearing being at peace with it. Accepting that death is a part of life and that it will come when it comes—there's no point in resisting it. This feels like a major turning point of sorts, another layer of consciousness experienced.

With releasing the fear of death comes releasing the need for things to be a certain way. When I no longer fear death, I no longer need to control how my life unfolds. I can experience greater trust and surrender. Fear of death is the ultimate fear that keeps us clinging to control, trying to keep ourselves alive and safe, unsure when we will take our last breath.

So much comes from this place of fear. It is very deeply rooted and very human. And no one can blame us—it is biological; it is our very nature. We believe we are here in this form in order to survive at all costs. And yet, when we can learn to no longer fear death—as is inevitable for each and every one of us—we can embrace our finiteness, releasing the need to ignore this reality. In doing so, we embrace another reality: we are infinite. Ultimately, there is nothing to fear.

Earlier, over lunch, Clint had asked me what my soul truly desires. "To be free," I said. A couple months ago, that looked like leaving my apartment and traveling somewhere. Being a nomad. Not being "tied down." It has only been in listening to that desire, making the decision to leave, and then later realizing I actually want to stay that I have been offered exactly what my soul truly desires—greater freedom! How? Because by going through this whole experience, I have gotten to practice non-attachment. As it says in the Tao Te Ching, "Without attachment, the wise man is liberated from aversion." I translate this to mean "free from care"—caring one way or the other about something. I was not actually attached to my ideal apartment or to what people would think. I was not attached to the lease I had signed or to the idea of leaving Sioux Falls. And, in the end, I am not even attached to what freedom needs to look like.

Releasing my attachment to all these things, I experience greater liberation. I may have stayed in Sioux Falls, moved downstairs to a smaller space, and continued my commitment to a lease. But, cultivating this feeling of carelessness, I see I am able to freely leap into the unknown.

Once we remember what and who we truly are, we don't need to know *how* everything will unfold, instead relaxing into the knowing that all is working for us. That all is exactly as it is meant to be. That there is nothing to control or fear or hold on to. We are part of something much larger than each of us. That's not to say we don't participate in it. That's not to say we don't play a part. It's just to say we don't need to control the game. And it's a benevolent game we're playing, so we don't need to worry.

So, here's what I commit to: I commit to following my heart. I commit to making clear decisions and choices in each moment and communicating those to others based on the clarity and knowledge I have at the time. Those choices and decisions may change—they very likely will change as I continue to be true to myself and the information around me. I commit to choosing without deliberating what my next step should be, no longer fearing I'll choose wrong.

PART 2

CHOOSING

CHAPTER 7

REMEMBERING
WHO I AM

With the smell of palo santo wafting through the air, I lie back on my mat and begin the breath sequence—two inhales, one exhale. The music and gentle voice of my facilitator guide me on my journey. Within a few minutes, my mind gets out of the way, my body knows what to do, and I am transported into other states of consciousness.

I have been attending my group breathwork practice every week for many months now. Since I began, so much has been revealed, expressed, and released. My intention during this particular breathwork session is to receive more love and abundance than I think possible. The thing is, many of us (myself included) are conditioned to only allow ourselves to receive a certain amount of what we truly desire. By the end of the session, I realize that an abundance of love flows to and through me without end if I allow it.

One way this abundance of love flows to and through me is through all the men with whom I connect. It seems this is one way the universe reminds me of who I truly am. My journey with men is an interesting one. I have carried a lot of shame (and at times pride) around my numerous relations and encounters with men. After being in long-term monogamous relationships with two men throughout my twenties (one of whom was my husband), by the age of thirty-one, I was single for the first time. I wasn't sure what to do with myself. Before meeting Michael about a year later, my cousin told me I needed to go on fifty first dates before I could "settle down" with anyone. Fifty?! That's a lot of work! How would I ever accomplish that? Well, I didn't, but I made good progress.

When I was still a consultant, I was traveling internationally for work and decided to allow myself the same freedom to explore various cities and countries as to explore various men. It all started with a Frenchman in Ireland. Then, there was a Greek soccer player in Belgium. I was surprised by how empowering it felt to have my first intentional one-night stand with a very young British man who was the bartender of my local pub in West Hampstead, London. As the countries got stamped in my passport, I collected various stamps on my heart.

In the year since Michael and I separated, though no longer interested in going on fifty first dates or online dating, I still have a deep desire for a partner. And I've been exploring what exactly that now means and looks like. I have attracted many men from all walks of life. Some younger; some older. Some single; some married. Some just passing through; some who I'd known from years past.

After breathwork, I go to lunch with a friend and discuss some of my recent escapades. I wonder if, at times, I avoid expressing or receiving love because I don't want the box I assume it comes in. I resist being "tied down," and so I don't express or receive love out of fear of that happening. Or I know a particular person isn't "the one," and so I refuse to express or receive love even for a night out of supposed respect for myself. What if it were possible to love another human being without the confines or restrictions or constraints of putting that love in a box? What if we were free to love another and express that love unconditionally without needing anything in return? What if the constraints of the label or the box hinder us from expressing true love in whatever shape or form it comes in?

I know label-free love is challenging for me because I so often become attached to the source of love (the person giving or receiving it) instead of remembering that the love is sourced from within and is simply being expressed to or through another. Someone else can remind me of that love within, and that feels so good. From there, I so quickly identify the other as the one who makes me feel that way rather than remembering that I have all this within me already and that this "other" simply offers me an opportunity to share and express it.

The next day, I receive an email from the facilitator. He shares some feedback from a group member that the way my body expresses itself during breathwork is distracting. While he is in no way scolding me, this message stings badly at first. I can easily go into my defensiveness and "higher than thou" attitude—and at first I do. I can feel my little girl protesting: "I thought I was allowing myself to be exactly who I am without judging myself or controlling myself? But, apparently, I distract others. Clearly, I need to modify my behavior. Why can't I just be and do me? Why do I have to change so others can feel more comfortable?"

"I hear you, little Amanda," my higher self says. "I see how committed you are to being yourself without judgment or control. I see how open you are to experiencing whatever you are going to experience. I see how openhearted and trusting you are of the process and the journey. Equally, this, too, isn't who you are. You are not how you respond to the active energy that moves through your body during a breathwork journey. You are not how you show up in this world. You are not this physical form or body. Yes, you desire to express yourself as fully as you can while in this form, *and* it is not who you truly are."

"But how do I then freely express myself in a way that feels true and authentic?" my little girl continues.

"Great question. By being open to all that comes to you. By checking in and seeing how it feels. By staying out of judgment—of yourself and others. By remaining open to this path. By remaining open to the various opportunities. By coming from a place of love at all times—for yourself and others. The reality is, this is who and what we are—love."

This inner dialogue helps me loosen my grip a bit more on my attachment to what others think. I can see how I want everyone to like me. But I have yet to love myself so fully and completely that I no longer identify with or need others' opinions of me. The concept of this kind of self-love sounds simple, yet in practice, I find it very challenging. Thanks to the support of my breath and the release of DMT in my brain the day before, though, I am getting greater clarity and awareness of what truly is. I refuse to see myself as less than or better than others. I refuse to see myself as wrong. In doing so, I am unable to see others as less than or better than me. I am incapable of seeing others as "wrong."

What this means for me is that I do not need to modify who I am to get others to like me (nor do I need to even when they don't)—let's be honest, sometimes even *I* don't like me. No matter how awesome I think I am, not everyone is going to like me. That is their choice. I will annoy *and* attract people. We all are this way. I don't need to act differently out of spite or the desire to impress. I am invited to stand even more firmly in the truth of who I am. I consider more deeply accepting that truth and reality—starting with myself. I am *all* of it. Isn't that what it means to be human? That we are *all* of it? That we'll possess and express qualities we like and don't like? And this goes both ways. Isn't it amazing how we are all just mirrors and reflections for one another?

I choose to see this as an opportunity. An opportunity to remember that none of this—how I choose to express myself, how I distract someone else, how active or relaxed my body is during breathwork, how many men I sleep with or who I am attracted to, what choices I make—is who "I am." In each and every moment, I am a completely new person—everyone is. I am offered a new opportunity to show up differently than I have before. I fully release myself and others from all guilt, shame, judgment, and condemnation. And this is an opportunity to show up differently to see if there is a greater benefit to be received as I let go of any lingering attachments to who I think I am. This is freedom.

When it comes to remembering who we truly are, there are stages. We begin at a very early age, repressing or denying or avoiding our "self" as a way of pleasing others, fitting in, or receiving love. We believe our natural desires and inclinations are not okay. We are told we are "too much" or "too loud" or "too slow." We spend many, many years in this stage of self-repression, afraid to be who we think we are lest we upset others.

Imagine you're a talented saxophone player. Playing the sax is loud—perhaps too loud and distracting to others around. So, you go years without playing, repressing and dismissing your desire out of fear. Perhaps the fear is of embarrassment or a scolding or attention. These fears are universal, but how they show up is individual. Either way, the saxophone isn't getting played.

At some point, many of us will begin the journey back to who we truly are, which means first reclaiming who we *think* we are. We might rebel or defend or act out in order to demonstrate who we "really are," wishing to swing in the opposite direction from all those years of trying to please others and stuff our own desires and gifts back in.

Let's say, one day, you're at a jam session where other people are picking up their instruments and playing. You pick up your instrument and begin to reclaim and remember who you are. You start playing. You play to your heart's content. You play loud and proud. You play riffs that no one else can play. You are shining.

By now, you start to feel pretty good. You are expressing your "true self." You are finally who you thought you always were. And over time, you start becoming attached to this new way of being in the world. You begin telling everyone about it and inviting them all to hear you play. You might even play in multiple groups all over. You talk about it all the time. You might even play some solo acts here and there. You are filled up as you are now "being you" and shining your light for all to see. There is nothing wrong with this. Yet this is not the end of the journey either. You have not now "arrived."

Let's now say that at some point, someone asks you to stop playing because you are distracting them. This upsets you. You now feel the need to defend yourself because this is "who you are." You don't want to now dim or deny the self you recently reconnected to. So you get defensive or angry. On the other hand, other people start praising you for your talents and your gifts. You become slightly inflated with all the praise. You now continue playing because of how much people like it. In either case, you've now become attached to this "self" that you reclaimed.

This is when you have the opportunity to let it all go. This is when you put the saxophone down for a bit. Not because playing is bad or wrong. Not because it's not okay to share your gifts and talents and "be who you are." But because it has now become yet one more thing you're attached to and no longer free of.

This is still an expression of who we think we are, not necessarily who we truly are, not where we are intended to "land." We think we are outgoing or determined or smart or gifted or creative or shy or successful or whatever. And we are all these things. Equally, when we truly remember that we are these things, we no longer need to go out defending them or showing them off. Getting here is a necessary part of the reclamation. We must embrace it as fully as we can. And then we must let it go.

I am realizing at rapid speed that my attempt to control things is done out of fear that if I don't, I will lose it. As I sit with this, it becomes clear that I do the same thing with myself. If I don't control who I think I am, if I fully let go, then I fear I will lose myself. While I sit on my couch reflecting on this email, I ask myself, "What am I afraid of losing?" and tears come to my eyes. "My personality. This thing I have worked so hard over all these years to create."

I think back to my past journeys with Ayahuasca, San Pedro, mushrooms, and, most recently, DMT. Each time I have used one of these plant medicines, I have experienced discomfort and a very real fear of losing control. Taking substances like these is scary because, being out of control, I feel I risk losing myself, either for a moment or irreversibly. But my life is not one guided by fear, so there has been an opportunity here for me. And each time I was reminded of how safe I ultimately am. Looking around my small, consciousness-expanding apartment, I am so grateful for the opportunities I have had to use psychedelics to continue shedding these layers.

It is hard to put words to mystical experiences, not adequately explainable with our limited vocabulary. But this is a book, after all, so I will do my best. Over the past three months, I have gone on three DMT journeys. If you aren't aware of what DMT is, it is the main chemical compound found in Ayahuasca and occurs in many plants and animals. It is also naturally created in our brains and can even be released during breathwork sessions. The thing I like most about it is how short of a trip it is, typically only fifteen minutes. But, wow, did I go deep. Each time I journeyed, I did so with a different man (who knew this would be such a strong theme in my life, to journey with so many different men—yet how apropos). One of them I had known for a day, the other two for a few weeks. Each one younger than the one prior, and each quite evolved and comfortable with psychedelics. I say this because I have felt safe in each and every case, even when we hardly knew each other.

The first trip of the three was total bliss. Going into it, I had no idea what to expect, and it completely blew my mind. I sat cross-legged on the floor in my kitchen across from Eric, the same guy I briefly considered moving to California with. Before he left town and I moved apartments, he offered to share his DMT with me, and I graciously accepted the invitation. We opened the container (both the one the DMT came in and the space for the sacred journey we were about to embark on—this is very common and important before undergoing this sort of experience), set intentions, and did some breathwork in preparation together. He loaded the pipe and handed it to me. I lit the bowl, inhaled deeply, and asked, "When will I kno——?" And off I went.

With my eyes wide open, I saw incredible shapes and colors all around me. My apartment became a Salvador Dalí painting. Eric's face transformed before my eyes. I touched my face to see if I was still real. I laughed a belly laugh of pure joy. I felt the interconnectedness and beauty of everything. After the feeling of timelessness dissipated, I came back. One thing I took away from the journey is how magnificent it all is and how I am a part of it. We have no idea what is really around us (or what reality is), yet we spend most of our lives trying to figure it out or get stuck in the need to know.

My second trip was quite different. I invited a different guy who I also had fallen hard for (yes, there's a pattern here) to join me. We had hooked up many times, had amazing sex and conversations, and even talked about doing a podcast together. This time, knowing what to expect actually brought up more anxiety. Like my first time, prior to starting, Brendan and I set the container and our intentions. Again, I went first, but I took more than I took the first time. At first, I was afraid I'd over-done it. I got nervous I was losing myself, so I focused on breathing and taking it all in. This trip gifted me an insight that I am totally safe, protected, and that I can never "overdo it." I am now more reassured that I can never lose myself, and, equally, I'm completely free to be more of me—there's no such thing as "too much." Well, isn't that a relief! This is what I love about mind-opening experiences such as this—I am reminded of what's true, not what my mind has had me believe.

My third trip occurred in the wee hours of the winter solstice just a few days ago with Caleb, a young man I met earlier that day. Unlike the other two, it was a completely impromptu and unplanned expe-rience, and it took place in my current apartment. He went first, and I "babysat" while he was in it. There is something so beautiful about watching another person experience this from a completely lucid place. Afterward, he told me that he could feel the Divine Feminine with him the entire time, even when he closed his eyes. Initially, I didn't fully understand what he meant. As I continue to embrace more of my feminine aspects, I see how integral it is for me to hold that energy for others, whether they are friends, clients, or lovers.

Once it was my turn, again not really knowing how much to take, I smoked the entire remainder. I imagine it wasn't that much, yet away I went again! Immediately, I was surrounded by colors and fractals. I believe I traveled to the astral plane. As soon as I "took off," I was free from my body, which was a new experience for me. It was slightly scary, though mostly beautiful. Whenever I felt overwhelmed, Caleb encouraged me to breathe, and I did. Once again, I found myself laughing those deep belly laughs from the exquisiteness of it all. Near the end, I needed help coming back down into my body. He koala bear-hugged me—it felt amazing. I crawled up onto his lap like a child and held on tight. Experiencing the connection with another human being, connecting and merging with another form, felt divine. As I came to, I had this revelation that my ego (my personality) is what keeps me alive here on this physical plane—without her, I would be gone. Her desire to be in this physical form brought me back to "reality." No wonder I'm afraid of losing her.

Having an "out of body" experience can feel scary because it connects us more deeply with our fear of losing ourselves, at least if we believe that we are only this body. Simultaneously, it assures us that we are far more than this body. These journeys have helped me loosen my grip on who I think my ego is and realize I can never lose it. I've come to realize we must first believe we are separate from our minds and our egos in order to heal. Yet the truest healing occurs when we heal the illusion of separation. In that moment, I gained a whole new appreciation for my ego as well as my physical form. This is what life is all about. This form. This physical plane. This is where we get to feel, create, connect, and love. I now understand why my shaman in Peru laughed all those years ago after I proudly shared I had buried my ego—she and I are truly one.

DMT helped me see how I find comfort, security, and protection by getting into my head and trying to make sense of things. While I am now clearer that I can never lose my "self," which I have spent so many years brilliantly and beautifully creating, I'm still afraid. How do I integrate this newfound awareness? It's a deeper experience of the same fear I felt traveling through California and writing my first book.

Preparing to welcome in a new year, in typical Amanda style, I want to get to the root of this fear. I start to cry, thinking the self I've cultivated can't coexist with this new, post-DMT self. That if I don't use my mind, I'll walk around ignorant, feeling disconnected and aloof. Obviously, though, it's not one or the other—I'm not *either* intelligent and capable of seeing things as they are *or* some dumb person who goes through life without a clue. I don't have to choose between them. But I can see how this personality I have created—this self that "always has the answers" and "always has it figured out" and is "always three steps ahead of everyone else"—is keeping me from feeling pain, protecting me from the extreme discomfort of not knowing. I acknowledge that the neurosis is there, and I am willing to be vulnerable and say, "You know, I don't know all the answers. I don't know why things are unfolding the way they are." But also, I *do* know: it's unfolding *for* me, and sometimes things just *are*.

During my weekly breathwork session the following Sunday, I experience pure non-separation. I hear from deep inside myself, "Nothing is wrong with you." I feel deep love, compassion, and wholeness within myself. There's nothing "wrong" with who I am or what I'm doing. There's nothing "more" that I need. I'm already exactly where I'm meant to be. I can now move through life with greater ease and trust. Some of us spend our whole lives traveling the world, ingesting substances, trying to "get there." Really, we have been "here" all along. What I'm learning is that my true power and strength are in the gentleness, the surrender. When we relax and let go of control, we experience a greater, deeper power from within.

Lying on my mat with the soothing sound of the singing bowl washing over me, my inner voice speaks again: "What if you just relaxed more?" I take this as a beautiful opportunity for me to explore other ways of experiencing stillness and deep samadhi. Going in even more. I lie still, letting go of the idea that even surrender needs to look or feel a certain way as I once thought. I notice how I am able to soften even more when I allow myself to feel secure in who I *truly* am and be me, whether that means being motionless or writhing around.

Like the story of the saxophone player, at the end of the day, no matter how gifted you are at playing the sax and how much joy it brings you and others, this is not who you truly are. This is simply who you "think you are." Ultimately, with this new recognition, you play the sax when you feel inspired to play the sax. Sometimes you choose to sit out and watch others play—no matter how "good" or "bad" they might be. You no longer feel the need to defend your ability or talents. Equally, you don't hide or suppress them. If someone hands you a saxophone to play, you might play it. If someone asks you to stop, you might stop. It doesn't matter either way. Because you are not a sax player. You are something much more, much deeper, much beyond that. You are the one who observes your ability to play the music so beautifully. You are the one who observes your ability to feel the desire to play the sax and not play it. You are all that which is witness to the music and the desire to create it. You are both the player and the instrument. You are the music itself and the silence. It is at this level of consciousness that you no longer suppress who you truly are or reclaim who you think you are but rather begin to live from the seat of who you have always been and always will be.

My intention for 2019 is to continue this journey to deeper trust and relaxation. This requires even more vulnerability, which isn't about sharing my feelings or expressing myself in a certain way. It's about being vulnerable enough to open to the flow of things (which means not knowing what will happen next). It's about being honest with myself and others, accepting who I am, and expressing what is scary and tender for me as it arises. And in so doing, releasing it, freeing more and more space around my heart to lead the way in order to remain open to this path and come from a place of love at all times.

By now, Awaken Village Press has published its first two books. Some more clients have said yes to working with me, and I am beginning to make a living doing what I love. As slow as that feels at times, I am gaining more confidence that I am doing exactly what I'm here to do. People are finding me through word of mouth and referrals. Everything is unfolding naturally and organically. I am excited about the synchronicity and support all around me. I am feeling in full alignment with what I'm here to do and offer. I am delighted by how resonant each person is with my worldview and where I am at on my journey when they start working with me. It is all so perfectly and divinely orchestrated.

I start to notice how my non-judgmental presence and love for my clients have created this safe space for them to share more fully and authentically. They tell me things they've never told others. I am able to reflect back to them their truth and remind them how important their story is so they feel free to share it with the world. I believe through the act of unconditional love, people can see who they truly are.

Much like how I desire to do this for my clients, I desire for men to realize their truth and feel free through the unconditional love of a woman. I believe there aren't enough men being loved unconditionally. I mean, there aren't enough people being loved unconditionally. And I desire to do that more often.

What if this is one of the reasons I'm here? What if this is one of the reasons I fall in love so easily? What if this is my saxophone? I realize more and more just how much love I have to give. I've begun to acknowledge and accept that I *am* love. But how do I love freely *and* have what I want—a single partner to love deeply for the rest of my life, who will create a child with me? This can be very confusing for someone who is looking for her "one and only." I'm not sure what to do with it.

I do not get to determine how this all turns out, which can be quite frustrating. What I get to choose is how I show up each and every day. How much I open (or close) my heart. How much love I allow to flow to and through me. How much I lean into the discomfort and space of expanding more into my heart, into my softness, into trust, into surrender, into vulnerability, into love.

CHAPTER 8

PUSHING & PULLING

In the light of the full moon in February 2019, I am inspired to write a thank-you note to my beloved. No, I am still not in a relationship with anyone, but I've done a lot of work and am very ready for him to arrive. Even though I've come to terms with the fact that there is no "magic being" who will only possess the qualities I want (and none that I don't), I'm still drawn to get clear on who I'm calling in. After all, a full moon is a time to honor where we're at, what has come to fruition, and what we desire to manifest.

It is the first time I've done this so intentionally when it comes to partnership. In the past, I haven't been very clear on what I wanted—I simply responded to what was put in front of me. Now, I am practicing consciously choosing what I want. Much like with my apartment, I figure I ought to start by getting clear on what I desire, writing it down, and then allowing it to come to me. And it does.

Starting the very next day, I attract a man who seems to match the "criteria" I have written down. This man, who lives in Canada, is an amazing father, financially stable, committed to his growth and evolution as a human, and takes care of himself physically and mentally. Rather quickly, I think I have met "him." I believe he could be my life partner. I feel a slight flutter in my heart, but I don't feel overly giddy as I have in the past. I am surprised by how grounded and true it feels. It "makes so much sense" and none at all. It is vulnerable to open my heart and choose in such a confident way—like, yup, I choose him. After all, I've spent a lot of time being afraid to choose lest I be wrong. But I do it anyway. In a matter of weeks, I tell him how I can see myself growing old with him. As much as he is enjoying getting to know me, he can't return the feeling with as much confidence.

It has me questioning—again—if I have learned to trust myself. Starting with Eric last year and then Brendan and now this Canadian, I change my mind so often, choosing a new person every month, it seems. And yet, I truly feel a soul connection *and* that I have found what I am looking for with each one. How can I be wrong so many times? But there it is: that belief that there is a "wrong." That belief that I am to choose a person and, if he doesn't choose me in return, I've made a wrong choice. I continue to get glimpses that this isn't how it works.

These experiences, at times, bring out my worry that I am incapable of being faithful or committed to one man. What if that's why I hadn't yet found my person? Am I capable of picking just one person for the rest of my life? I feel torn in two. My soul continues to make it known that it wants exactly that, yet my personality continues to worry it will be disappointed or find something "better" in a matter of time. How do I choose one and still love all?

It's not that I desire to have multiple partners or want to continue adding stamps in my passport, so to speak. I am open, but I am selective in love, friendship, and work. I desire to love those I am here to love and serve those I am here to serve. So, how in the world do I express that and be that without becoming attached to the object of my love or desire (or trying to manipulate or control it)?

We can all push and power our way through life to get what we want. For a long time, I have looked at my power as my ability to know certain things or make certain things happen, making things manifest. It's all control, control, control. Many of us fear that if we let go of control, we will lose our power. After all, I feel powerful when I get what I want, like the Greek man in Brussels or my perfect apartment. In reality, I wasn't "in control" in either case—Andreas approached me from across a crowded dance floor of hundreds of people, and my building just so happened to have a unit available for me to move into. But here's the thing: in both situations, I made it clear what I wanted—I made eye contact with Andreas and gestured him over with my hand, and we all know how I manifested my apartment.

I still believe deep down that, much like freedom and surrender, standing in my power has to look a certain way, like some sort of superhero as opposed to who I am at all times—unapologetically, confidently, assuredly—knowing that I am whole, complete, and worthy. Equally, I have feared my power and what I am capable of making manifest. If I'm in control of all this, then fuck. I haven't always manifested what I want. So I figure I'll try something new.

Continuing to navigate various dynamics with men (and with my own power), I start to notice the difference between being vulnerable or "sharing my truth" from a place of control and from a place of grounded knowing. At times, I have refrained from sharing my deep knowing or directly telling someone how I feel. I find myself sharing some of it and then holding back other parts out of fear. It seems like if I declare what I truly desire and share that truth, I'm in some way taking away their ability to choose (or pushing them away). This comes from years of believing that I manipulate and control others, which is actually a mistaken belief regarding the power I have (and some karmic debt of having misused and abused my power in the past, most likely). I have also feared that if they reject me, I won't be able to handle it.

And sometimes, I *have* shared my truth from a place of manipulation, thinking I could control the outcome by saying how I felt. It's a cluster. Perhaps I have been uncomfortable about something, so I "speak my truth" in order to receive something from someone in return, hoping to feel better. A lot of these fears and questions have been rooted in the fear and belief that if I don't [fill-in-the-blank], I'll lose him or won't get what I want. If I don't tell him how I feel, he won't know and might not have the courage to love me in return. If I don't send the message, I might never see him again. If I don't get clear on exactly what I'm calling in, what I want will pass me by.

Now, vulnerable truth (saying "I love you" or "I can see myself growing old with you" or "You are everything I want in a man") may feel scary and a little crazy, depending on when it's offered (like on the first day we meet), but it isn't necessarily shared in order to control or manipulate the situation. I can share my truth without aiming to influence an outcome but rather to speak what I feel in the moment (remembering that it can change in another moment). And this isn't only in regards to speaking my truth; it also includes following my heart's desires in all ways. To me, what feels most vulnerable is remaining open and going with the flow, which also means flowing with what desires to be expressed as it desires to be expressed. And, as I'm seeing more and more, just because I follow my heart doesn't mean I get to control the outcome of that expression.

As I practice being more vulnerable in this way, my familiar doubts and fears rear their ugly heads. Leading from the heart isn't easy. True freedom is an inside job; it doesn't matter how free we are in the external world if we are still imprisoned by our thoughts, beliefs, and narratives. I must continue to surrender. Trust. Open up, and then open some more. I mean, it's one thing to surrender to myself, knowing that I need not control who I am for fear of losing her. It's a totally different thing when it comes to the fear of losing others. I am so afraid that even after surrendering control, I will still feel heartbroken and disappointed whenever something once again doesn't work out. I'm so afraid that I will get my hopes up only to have them come tumbling down around me, whether that has to do with falling in love or meeting a client I'm excited to work with.

As the snow continues to fall almost into March, I have a talk with myself about my feelings and how they're *always* true, even as they change. Just because I don't feel the same way now about someone or something as I had before (or those feelings aren't returned) doesn't mean it is false or "wrong." The outcome doesn't minimize or delegitimize my feelings. So, that must mean I can always trust myself! Wow. What a freeing realization. I no longer need to be afraid that if my feelings change (which they might) or the person who elicits them changes (who also might), I am (or they are) not to be trusted. Ultimately, what I am experiencing is love, which is the core of who I am. How can that ever be false or wrong?

While I see more evidence to trust myself and how I feel, I still don't understand why I keep meeting these men who I deeply believe are "the one." Why I have this deep connection with each of them only to be left disappointed time after time. It doesn't make sense. I continue to receive these winks from the universe that I've met "him," and then that's it. I know we meet every person for a reason, season, or lifetime—but I keep getting hung up on why it isn't a lifetime yet.

For someone who loves to find meaning in everything, letting go and not needing to understand the meaning of something feels very unsettling. I can't walk down the street without seeing a sequence of numbers or a phrase or an item or a person that offers me confirmation or validation of something. I move through life, seeing signs and synchronicities everywhere I turn. This gives me comfort. This offers me peace of mind. I feel supported and taken care of in these moments. I know I am on the right path and am doing what I'm "meant to do." This I love more than anything—that nod from the universe saying, "Yes, this way. Yes, you know what you want, and you're heading in the right direction." It's my source of external validation. It's my way of knowing I'm choosing correctly. And, as frustrating as it is, I feel this same validation as I experience these soul connections.

At times, I can see the absurdity of my search for meaning, especially when it comes to numbers. You have no idea how often I notice numbers on license plates or check totals or times on a clock or important dates. Numbers are significant to me, so that's how the universe most often converses with me. They're showing up for a reason, right? And so I can't disregard them. I hear my inner knowing say, "You create what you want, so be clear on what you want—because you'll get it." This is something I'm still wrestling with. Am I creating these signs? Or are they showing up to guide me? Or is it both? How do I create what I want without being in control?

As my birthday approaches and the South Dakota winter continues with no end in sight, a friend invites me to join her in Costa Rica for a festival. It would be the longest trip I've ever taken alone, and tropical paradise sounds like a heavenly way to celebrate my thirty-seventh birthday (which adds up to ten and is a number signifying completion). My intention is to be love and light with every individual I encounter. After all, that's what I am and why I'm here on this earth. What a way to celebrate my existence—being more of who I am! I begin my trip by asking myself: "What if, when traveling, instead of overplanning and worrying about the details, I remain open to the flow of life and all the miracles that will come my way?"

And boy, do they come! I receive sign after sign that I am being guided and taken care of. That I am exactly where I am meant to be. I choose to see each sign as validation. I experience this plethora of synchronicities and miracles when I choose to let go of control and let life guide me. A tourist wants to get away from the familiar but not go anywhere "new," sticking to what's planned out and within their comfort zone. A traveler wants to experience new things, often unplanned, and is open to what happens. The tourist exerts more control; the traveler trusts the nature of things. I am most certainly a traveler.

My trip begins at 8:00 a.m. (my life path number) on 3/3 in 2019, which also adds up to 3 (2+0+1+9=12; 1+2=3). Three is a very significant number to me, being both the number of my birth day and month. On the first leg of my flight, I am "randomly" assigned seat 33. The flight number adds up to 11 (another very significant number in my life, and also 8 + 3), and the plane is an Airbus 321 (3 and 2 + 1 = 33).

One of the last passengers to board my connecting flight to LAX after many others are forced to check bags, I walk right on with my carry-on, with plenty of space above and around my seat for the over four-hour flight. Once in Costa Rica, I take a taxi to my Airbnb, another "random" choice. I know nothing about the area and trusted my inner guidance when choosing where I would stay for ten nights. I arrive at the intersection of Avenida 3 and Calle 3 to what's more a palace than a house. Later, I learn that my host, Michael (like my previous partner, guru, and the everpresent archangel who seems to make itself known to me in many forms), met his partner, Elisabeth, on this very corner exactly 11 years ago. Yes, I know, it's getting ridiculous.

This Michael, a seventy-something year-old German man, is one of the most fascinating people I have ever met. It takes him a couple of days to warm up to me, but once he does, we share many things with each other. He was very good friends with Tim Leary, a man well-known for his work with psychedelics (and someone I have heard a lot about over the past few years). As someone who listens to a lot of Ram Dass, this felt like two degrees of separation as he and Tim Leary also ran in the same circles. Here I am, staying at this particular individual's large house on the coast of Costa Rica for two weeks "by chance." Most evenings, we spend sitting on the balcony drinking chilled red wine (this is how they do it in Costa Rica), engaging in heart-opening and mind-opening (and, at times, mind-bending) conversations. Michael speaks with the same sort of authority, clarity, and levity as Ram Dass does in the numerous lectures of his I've listened to by this point. Just speaking with him at times feels like a psychedelic trip.

"It's all an illusion," he reminds me during one of our conversations. "And how do illusionists work? They make us believe something. Their entire illusion is founded on beliefs. Change what you believe and you change the illusion. That's how you change reality. When we change the belief that we are separate, we change the illusion of separation. And since we are ultimately not separate, we have absolutely nothing to lose."

This is what I got a glimpse of during my DMT journey, and it still hits me like a ton of bricks. What have I been so afraid of for all these years, then? It isn't the only occasion when he offers me a perspective that intrigues or perplexes me. He reminds me that I'm not creating but rather registering, observing all of this. The one who is aware is who I Am. Again, what am I so worried about if I'm not even creating this?

"Are you a researcher?" he asks one day.

"No," I answer easily.

"To re-search means to search again. Searching for how things connect, finding additional 'proof' and support," he clarifies.

In that case, I am a re-searcher. He has pegged me well. I am slightly conflicted about this reflection, though. I'm fed up with constantly searching for how things connect, making sense of things—I'm trying to detach from this part of who I am. Then, he reminds me it's all a game, and we get to choose how we play the game (or dance the Lila, to use Ram Dass's words). We get to decide if we play the game or are played by the game.

One evening as Michael and I sit on the porch, he challenges something I hold near and dear to my heart. "There is no such thing as miracles; it all is just the way of things, the nature of things. There is no differentiation. That is the end of suffering and the experience of bliss. It's all bullshit, and it's all grace."

I look up at the stars, Orion in all his glory, as more tears flow from my eyes in awe and gratitude. After the two-hour conversation, all I can do is sit on the floor in my room, crying and laughing. This is bliss, or *ananda*. I used to think bliss means extreme happiness. The origin is Germanic for "blithe": "showing indifference." Seems awfully similar to how "secure" comes from "free from care" or "not caring." It all points to being free of concern because it all just is.

Bliss is all of it simultaneously. Joy *and* sorrow. Because all is the same. Equally, it is ineffable; one must experience it firsthand. I have touched this state a handful of times with plant medicine and during breathwork, resulting in this simultaneous laughing and crying. And now, apparently, I don't even need a cultivated setting or intense stimuli to recreate it. I am in deep gratitude for my entire journey and what Michael has shared with me during these ten days.

On my last evening, he sends me off with one more meaningful reflection. I am invited to join him and Elisabeth for dinner to thank me for my contribution to the enjoyment of the past couple of weeks. I don't quite know what he means—I haven't done anything special. Over dinner, he explains that my presence alone is my contribution. I am deeply moved.

After leaving the palace, I spend a week at the nearby retreat center that my San Francisco friend invited me to. It's my first music festival, but it is so much more than that. Appropriately named Sound & Silence, it is a week of just that, where about 200 of us come together to dance, sing, breathe, and so much more.

Over the course of six days, I connect with myself and others in ways I haven't before. My tent is next to a woman who lives on the Caribbean side in a beach town called Puerto Viejo. She is working on a book, and we talk about what it might look like to work together on bringing her book into the world. She even gifts me the encouragement to host my own writer's retreat.

I make friends with a young woman originally from Switzerland, living with a man in the Diamante Valley who is working on his first book, a spiritual allegory. She virtually introduces us, resulting in my first Costa Rica-based client and a reason to return in the future. These are the first of a number of divine connections that reveal themselves to me over my time here.

Time expands and slows down for me while I am in Costa Rica. It could be the land. It could be my state of being. It could be that I've reconnected with souls that help me remember time is an illusion. As my host Michael shared with me about time and zooming out, when we stop for a couple days, we're still consumed with the small details of life. When we take a week, we begin to expand our thinking to larger tasks or ideas. When we take a month, we begin to think of people around us or larger-scale questions. Take more than that and you begin to ask what's the meaning of life. The more we stop, the more we can zoom out to what's truly important. We are surrounded by minute-by-minute updates, news, and notifications that, ironically, give us only a very small view. Paradoxically, this keeps us from being present. The more present we are, the bigger the picture becomes.

On the last day of the gathering, I meet a man with whom I feel a deep soul connection. Immediately, I tell him how I feel (no surprise there!). As a good traveler does, I've intentionally left some space at the end of my trip for spontaneous plans to be made. With a little hesitation as he explains he just started dating someone a few weeks ago, Rodolfo welcomes me to stay in his second bedroom for my last few days in the country. While eyegazing together on his couch (you know, as you do), he tells me we've shared past lives together. Despite his current circumstance, I desire to share this life together. He embodies so much of what I imagine my beloved will.

While we connect on a spiritual level and through playing music together, he keeps very clear boundaries that I, reluctantly, honor. As much as I respect someone's ability to set boundaries and my ability to honor them, doing so can be hard when I feel such a strong pull. What if our connection in that way is the thing that clarifies if I am his person or she is? Yes, I see this is still my desire to control things. Simultaneously, I am so grateful he is a man of integrity and I am able to meet him there. This is something I deeply value, and I appreciate that it is showing up more clearly in my life as a reflection of who I am becoming. After a number of conversations, I receive clear guidance that I am to vulnerably express what desires to be expressed and release the rest.

While having my last lunch in Costa Rica with Rodolfo, I summon the courage to speak my truth. "I have a deep knowing that my beloved and I are to journey together, co-creating, serving, and contributing to the New Earth. I believe he is you. And I choose you." It is still scary to say that because there is still some part of me that worries I am wrong. But what if I am? Then, at least, I am clearer on what I desire, and I'm claiming it and making it known. "And if it isn't you, then I can lovingly release you and know he is close behind."

Awaiting his response as the waiter chooses this exact moment to bring us our bill, Rodolfo takes out his card to pay. I take a few deep breaths as the untimely transaction takes place. Trusting myself enough to speak my truth in this way is a big deal to me. I feel my confidence in my self, in my being-ness. Even when speaking my truth feels scary or vulnerable, it's simply because I'm not familiar with doing it. So, I take the chance to practice. I lean in and trust more than I have before. Being vulnerable or speaking my truth is no longer about controlling or manipulating my environment. Instead, I am choosing to say what I feel is true because anything else would feel uncomfortable and completely out of integrity. As I say these words, I remember that I can't control his decision and I can handle whatever the outcome may be. No matter what occurs, it is a lesson for my soul.

He gently reiterates that he is committed to the woman he recently started dating and is not open to other options. I allow the emotions to pass through me, starting in my feet and making their way up to my eyes. I feel angry that I once again found the thing I want and am too late, so it passed me by. It pokes at my deep fear of missing what is meant for me if I don't act quickly.

I feel the nausea and hear the thoughts that arise. "I can't trust myself!" and "Can I know anything?!" As much as I meant what I said, some part of me must have still unconsciously believed that because I want this man and declare it so authentically, I will get him. Apparently, I still believe I can control the outcome of something with my behavior. That, if I choose him, he'll choose me. I mean, I believe this guy is my person, my beloved. I am tempted by long-familiar thought patterns: How in the world do I "get what I want" and make choices if I don't actually know anything? Then, I catch myself. "Remember, this is what it's all about—we can't ever know anything in the way we think we know it." With an exhale, I soften into my wisdom as we stand to leave.

As he drives me to the airport, I reminisce about the past few weeks. I haven't traveled around the country taking in all the immense beauty and diversity and adventure that it has. Instead, I have taken a deep journey within. I have explored parts of myself I hadn't yet explored. I've released further layers that no longer serve me. I've reconnected with nature and *my* true nature. I've glimpsed my future. I'm more secure in who I am and what I am here for. I've opened myself to greater possibilities and opportunities. I feel such immense gratitude for this life and the interconnectedness of it all. I have trusted in ways I've never trusted before. I've relaxed in ways I've never relaxed. I've witnessed myself not needing to know or understand or have an answer. There's something about spending time in a country where people speak another language that has reminded me again how I do not need to understand everything.

I see it everywhere around me: it's okay not to know. There's something deeper going on. I've allowed myself to be guided and trust the flow, no matter the outcome. I have experienced miracle after mundane miracle. Or, as Michael might say, I have experienced the nature of things again and again and again.

On the flight home, reflecting on all the clarity I've received and connections I've made, specifically with this man I knew from another life and all he said to me, I write in my journal. *I'm an inTERdependent woman. No shame or fear about that anymore. I need you as much as you need me. Together, we go higher. Our support for one another takes the other higher. Dependence is one-sided (I need you). Independence is also one-sided (I can do it without you). Interdependence is balanced (we need each other). I'm empowered and capable of taking care of myself,* and *my path includes walking beside another. This, I am clear on. I am solid in what I want and who I want, and I allow it to unfold. The love of my life is here, and I am ready for him. I've already chosen him. He's already chosen me. Now, it's just a matter of time.*

I remind myself that I *can* trust myself (and all that is). My truth has not misled me. My knowing has not changed. I know what I want. I want to journey with another along this path. This is true and unchanging. I can now see how my truth has actually remained constant, even while the players and characters around me shift. I trust that the partnership I am meant to have in this lifetime is on its way to me at the perfect time. And each time it isn't "him," then releasing him will inevitably make space for what I truly want.

In an attempt to reconnect to what I am calling in, I lie on my bed reading over the thank-you note I had written for my beloved over a month ago. With tears streaming down my face, I realize this letter is for me—it describes everything I love about myself, as well as what I desire. I know my partner is a perfect reflection of who I am and how I love myself. Whoever it is will be all that I am.

A question comes to me, begging an answer: What if I always get what I want, and it simply comes in forms that may not always seem like it at the time? This seems like such an obvious truth, yet it is hitting me for the first time, at least at this level. Thinking of it like this, I literally feel as though there's no way I *don't* get what I want. I simply need to be clear on what that is (and even if I'm not super clear, it will be made known to me because there is no alternative) and then trust that all is unfolding exactly as it's meant to.

"All life is an act of faith and an act of gamble," Alan Watts expresses so eloquently as I listen to one of his talks on YouTube. "But this is the most important thing that can be done: surrender. … And love is an act of surrender to another person." I relax further into this deeper knowing. It's interesting how trusting he's on his way can free me to love with more openness and non-attachment. Well, at least that's the idea! I know I have a ways to go in more deeply understanding the larger lesson: When it comes to love and partnership, my true power is not in taking control or showing how strong I am. It is in my softness, vulnerability, and receptivity.

CHAPTER 9

CHOOSING & LOSING

Enjoying the sun on my face, I'm walking through downtown Sioux Falls to meet my parents for Father's Day brunch when I see him. He looks so familiar even though I know I haven't met him before. Our eyes lock momentarily as we each continue walking our separate directions. We both catch each other turning back for a second look.

I arrive at the restaurant a few blocks down and am seated at a table on the sidewalk, where I wait for my parents to arrive. Within moments, that same guy walks up and sits at a nearby table. My parents arrive, and we sit together for over an hour, enjoying our celebratory family brunch. The whole time, I am aware of this intriguing man sitting by himself nearby.

I go to pay the bill, and the waitress tells me that the nice-looking gentleman at the other table has already paid it. What a lovely surprise and generous thing to do for a total stranger! I take the opportunity to go over and introduce myself.

He tells me his name—Michael (yes, another one). He lives in Vicenza, Italy, and is only in town for a couple weeks for work. I recognize this pattern in my life of meeting people at inopportune times, amplifying my deep-seated fear that what is meant for me might pass me by. I feel my old compulsion come up and temporarily debate which type of my power I wish to step into for this one. I want to give him my number or ask him for his. I want to be sure I have a way of contacting him or seeing him again. For the first time, I hear a voice in my head say, "If you're meant to see him again, you'll see him again." Even though I don't want to leave it up to chance like that, I choose to practice this new way of being, so that's exactly what I do.

I leave the restaurant, and within minutes, I receive a message from the waitress, who happens to be an acquaintance of mine. Michael had returned to ask her to pass his number along to me. I am over the moon that he took the lead. And while I may be practicing not being in control, I am still going to respond to what life presents me. Without delay, I send him a message. I am not one to sit on things, especially when it comes to matters of the heart. He asks what I'm doing, and I explain my plans to go to my sister's house for a Father's Day cookout. I welcome him to join us, and he writes, "Okay."

He meets us there, and we spend the entire day diving deep into meaningful conversation. I find myself surprised by how deeply we connect across so many topics we have in common. We discuss metaphysics, Alan Watts, philosophy, spirituality, and the mala bead bracelet on his wrist. I have certainly had other experiences of feeling a deep, soul connection with a man—even as recently as a few months ago—but something about this feels different.

When he kisses me under the light of the full moon (yes, we meet on a full moon), I feel electricity shoot through my body. I have an instantaneous vision of two people standing on a beach wearing white, and tears fill my eyes. I had just read a meme earlier that day about this full moon and its power to bring the energy of expansion and bigger vision. Expect new and surprising possibilities and invest your energy in healing yourself, it said. The perfect ground to let myself move into this final phase of letting go.

When he drops me off at home, I invite him inside. He declines, and I walk inside feeling overjoyed I've met this man and frustrated the night has come to an end. Standing in my living room, I feel compelled to go outside and see if he's still there. I return to my front porch just as he is turning the car around, coming back toward my place. He pulls over, gets out of the car, and walks up to me. "Okay," he says.

We walk inside, and he tells me about a cathedral he consciously took note of on his flight in, feeling a pull to it. With a smirk on my face, I say, "Oh, you mean the one just two blocks away?" He smiles back and points out a book on display in my apartment—*Be Here Now* by Ram Dass—and tells me he felt drawn to and picked up the exact same book at Barnes & Noble earlier that afternoon. We sit down and get deep in conversation about psychics and pendulums and oracle cards, and I ask if he'd like to draw a few. The four he draws bring another smile to my face, a rapidness to my heartbeat, and a slight shudder of fear: Mother Mary "Expect a Miracle," Kuan Yin "Compassion," Mary Magdalene "Unconditional Love," followed by Guinevere "True Love." I mean, really?! While eyegazing (this time on my couch), Michael also tells me about the past lives we've shared together. Every cell and inch of my body confirms this is true. It all feels like validation that we are connected on a soul level, that we weren't, in fact, meeting for the first time.

Eventually, we say good night, both a bit tense by the constraints of his circumstances, and he leaves. My mind is racing. While he carries the same name, this man is very different from my other Michael. And in many ways, he's very much the same. While very stable in comparison, he is unavailable in his own ways. He is married with children (though he's been thinking of getting a divorce, he can't imagine leaving his children). It's definitely not ideal—again, have I missed what is meant for me? Am I too late? He also wears layers of energetic armor to keep him safe and distant. He may not have spent any time in literal jail, but he often feels like a prisoner of his life.

By now, I have begun to look at this pattern of attracting unavailable men differently. I don't necessarily believe patterns are to be avoided but rather embraced and ventured into. I feel they are how we prepare for the thing our soul is guiding us toward. They are how we grow and expand as we align with our soul's desires. Perhaps my soul has always known I would be with a man who is initially unavailable, and all these years of practice and learning how to be patient and love unconditionally have occurred in order to prepare me.

On Michael's final evening in Sioux Falls, we get drinks on a patio overlooking the river and share a lovely dinner at one of my go-to spots downtown. Our dinner includes dessert, and yet, once we finish and pass by my favorite parlor, he suggests we stop for ice cream, which delights me. This man definitely knows the key to my heart. As the night comes to an end, he walks me home and we say goodbye. I'm a wreck. I don't want it to end. Here I am experiencing everything I want, and I'm about to lose it. He explains how he needs to be fully present with his life back home. He's unhappy with the state of his relationship and envisions a transition will take place that demands his attention. He requests that we refrain from communication as he continues to navigate it. As much as I don't want that, I understand and agree. He leaves, and I sit on my couch and cry. I cry big, fat tears. I grieve the loss of someone I just met but know so deeply. There are no guarantees I will ever see him again. If we speak again, it will be up to him. If I see him again, it will be up to him. If he becomes available, it will be up to him. My impulse to control isn't even an option.

The next day, feeling the weight of an emotional hangover, I'm standing in my kitchen making lunch when I hear an inner voice say, "Go to the airport." I know he is leaving for Italy this afternoon, but none of the specifics. I have no idea what time his flight is or which airline he's flying. Finding him would be nearly impossible. And even if I did, what was I supposed to do? Still, I listen to the directive. Without a car, I'm not sure how I'll get there. I call my mom, who just "happens" to be in my neighborhood. She can pick me up in ten minutes. How convenient. The voice urges me to bring a copy of my book, of which I just happen to have one left, and sign it for him.

Within half an hour, my book in hand and utter perplexity in my mind, I walk through the sliding glass doors to the check-in counters of our regional airport. There he is, standing twenty feet away from me. I can barely believe it. I walk up and tap his shoulder, startling the bejeezus out of him. Neither one of us had expected this moment, especially him. I smile, hand him my book, and wish him a safe flight. I don't know what else to do. I have no idea what he's thinking as he says, simply and awkwardly, "Thank you," and takes my book. He seems to be in shock, so I turn around and walk away. I want to say more or do more, but there's nothing more to do. I want him to ask me to stay, have a coffee, get on the plane with him, I don't know. Or even say "to hell with it" and miss his flight for just one more afternoon together. None of these things happen.

I get back in the car, simultaneously disappointed and elated that I heeded my intuition and got to see him one more time. There is no doubt in my mind that we were destined to meet again in this lifetime. From the moment I met him, I've gotten to feel what it's like to let go of controlling the outcome, relax, and trust more deeply. His appearance in my life offers me an opportunity to stand in my knowing and reclaim my authentic power—the alignment of my personality with my soul. As usual, it doesn't always feel good, but the whole experience is a gift. A gift of love. A gift of truth. A gift of synchronicity. A gift reminding me that I am on my path.

Equally, meeting this man has put me in the position to make a choice. It feels important that, if we are to be together in this lifetime, I believe we will have to choose each other—and that wouldn't be easy, given the life he has already chosen and my aversion to choosing things. Nonetheless, I hold to this belief that the choice will need to be made, eventually, and that this is the only option.

I'm no psychic (hence why I hire them), but I hold the intention that we will see each other again soon. I am again being asked to let go while holding on (to my vision, to my knowing). "How is that even possible?!" one part of me thinks. Still, I am committed to trusting my inner knowing even though it isn't always easy to uphold or embody. I have a long road ahead of me, and doubt will surface time and time again. Meeting this man has helped me deepen my faith in myself, fine-tune my ability to act from the seat of my soul, and listen (even when that sounds like a voice in my head). So, I decide to put that into practice even more. I start to listen a bit more closely to what my heart is saying. I become even more open to receiving messages and guidance.

Within days of him leaving, I start feeling a strong call to Italy. Ever since a quick weekend trip to Milan when I was still a consultant working in Ireland, I've wanted to go back. I mean, who doesn't like the idea of traveling to one of the most beautiful countries in the world? But is this just for him? I mean, he did make it clear that he has some major things to sort out in his life. And who knows how long that will take. So, why travel nearly 5,000 miles right now? Per usual, I see signs left and right confirming my knowing that I am to go. As I receive them, I continue to pay attention to what my heart is saying and where I am being guided. It feels significant that I be there during Lion's Gate on the 8th of August, less than two months away.

While walking to my favorite coffee shop one morning, I figure I would give something new a try and speak to my guides directly. I ask to receive a clear, undeniable sign as to whether I should go to Italy. As much as I desire to go and potentially see this man I feel such a deep connection with, traveling halfway across the globe because my soul told me to seems crazy. Remembering how the psychic advised me to listen to myself, I am still terrified of making the "wrong" choice or that I'm forcing something in some way. Am I once again taking the reins and chasing rather than following? Am I choosing to go to Italy because it is my heart's desire and I feel guided, or am I trying to control my destiny? Is there a difference? I don't feel sure anymore.

I struggle to know the difference between me just doing the next thing and trying to exert control. It brings up a lot of the things I've been exploring since going to Costa Rica and sitting with Ayahuasca all those years ago in Peru. Am I the chess master or the pawn? Or both?

While waiting for my matcha latte with coconut milk, a woman strikes up a conversation with me. We talk about her home country of England and how much we both love London and traveling. She's in Sioux Falls visiting her daughter. I grab my drink when it's ready, wish her a nice day, and start to walk away. "But there's nothing like Florence," she says suddenly. I stop and turn around. "That's where my husband and I got married." I feel I have received my clear sign. Still, I want to know if I am supposed to go to Vicenza specifically. Again, why would I choose to go to a small city that I've never heard of for any reason other than this man? I want confirmation that it is safe to trust my knowing and choose this.

At the airport the following week, I run into a former professor and his wife. They ask me where I'm going. I tell them I'm going to visit a couple of friends, first in North Carolina and then Connecticut, and am actually planning to go to Italy after that. One thing I've learned over the years is the power of living something into reality before it even happens.

"Oh, we love Italy," the professor's wife chimes in. "We go there every summer to see my sister. She works in Vicenza." My jaw nearly hits the floor. It's the first time I'm hearing anyone else mention this town's name. I guess this is the further confirmation I've been looking for. So, what now? Do I go all that way even if I might not see him? And if I do see him, what will he think? What if I spend money on this and need it for something else? What if I end up hurting someone—this man, his wife, or myself?

All this has me questioning my relationship to commitment ... again. Am I afraid of commitment, or am I actually learning what it feels like to commit to something or someone? What does that even look like? Am I willing to commit to someone who is unavailable? Who I have no communication with? Who I'm not even sure I will ever be with? Am I willing to commit to something without knowing how long it could take? Am I willing to commit to what I know to be true, to live the life I'm here to live and follow my soul's calling? What if I choose to go to Italy, no matter the outcome? What if I choose this man despite the facts known to me? I realize how insane that might look or sound, but it's essential for me to choose, to commit to something without being attached to the how or when. I am ready to "wait and see."

Finally, after tremendous hemming and hawing, multiple discussions with friends and mentors, and playing out the "worst-case scenario," I make my choice. I buy a one-way ticket to Venice and book a couple nights in Vicenza. I will figure out the rest once I get there. I'm still not sure if I'll be there for a few days or a few weeks. I want to experience

Venice, Tuscany, and Rome. I want to eat pasta and sit in piazzas and drink wine. I want to feel like Elizabeth Gilbert. It feels significant that I have met someone who lives in Italy, and perhaps, one of the reasons we met was to inspire me to travel there. After all, a reason, a season, or a lifetime.

Even though I am clear about what I am choosing, I do my best to release expectations and attachment to this trip being for him, seeing instead how it very much is for me. Still, I want to let him know I am coming. I would love the opportunity to see him again—this time in the country known for love. But I have no idea if he will even want to see me. Without a way to contact him by phone, I send him an email (which I have since he signed up for my newsletters after leaving Sioux Falls, thanks to the copy of my book I gave him). I let him know I will be arriving in Venice in a couple of days, not knowing if he will see it or respond. Either way, I feel immense gratitude for him, the catalyst for my adventure to see what experiences and gifts await me. But I am putting a lot on the line—my desires, my inner knowing, hundreds of dollars, not to mention how he'll react once he finds out I've taken this trip.

On August 1, I board my flight to Venice at JFK. Flying thousands of feet in the air, I ask myself: Are you okay if things don't turn out as you desire? My answer: yes. I never know what the outcome will be, and I no longer will live life based in fear. From here on out, the only thing I know is that love (my heart) is leading me, and I will follow that. The rest will be what it is. I can handle anything. Heartbreak, sadness, loss, financial impact. I can handle it all. What I can't handle is not trusting myself any longer.

When I land at Marco Polo airport, I have a response from him. He is surprised, to say the least. He was planning to be out of town with family this weekend, but things changed suddenly, and now they're going with their mom. He is unexpectedly available. "Dinner tomorrow night?" he writes. "I can pick you up."

I can hardly believe it. I mean, on the one hand, I'm familiar by now that this is what happens when I follow my heart and trust the nature of things. On the other hand, it is utterly incredible to me that it is actually working out this way, with so little planning or orchestrating, especially as I learn he is leaving the country for work in just a few days.

Taking the water taxi to my Airbnb in Venice, I am captivated by "the Floating City." It is unlike anything I have seen (other than in movies). It is breathtaking. I miraculously find my way to my Airbnb through the winding streets of Venice, rolling my suitcase behind me every clackety step along the way. Once I have my bearings, it's nearly dinnertime for Italians, which means it was getting quite late. I find a cute pizzeria with the cliché red and white checkered tablecloths, which both delights me and has me rolling my eyes. Tomorrow can't come soon enough, as this city is overflowing with couples and lovers everywhere I turn.

After spending my one night in Venice, I make my way to Vicenza and get settled in my next Airbnb. As promised, he picks me up and takes me to a lovely dinner in another town. It feels surreal to see him again after more than a month of no contact. Yet here he is, in the flesh. Just as I remembered him. Tall, handsome, the embodiment of masculinity. The epitome of what I'm looking for in a partner. He opens doors for me, beginning with the car. As he did in Sioux Falls, he pays for everything. He treats me like a queen. After an incredible dinner, a walk over the town's iconic bridge, and a drive around nearby Marostica, he drops me off, and we say our goodbyes. As much as I long for more, it feels noteworthy and important that we have such a strong connection without having a physically intimate one.

The next morning, still floating a bit, I walk to Piazza dei Signori, where Palladio's well-known basilica is located. I am immediately enchanted by the architecture and the colors and the energy of the entire place. The combination of cobblestone streets, marble statues, brightly painted houses all nestled together one after the other, along with the clambering of espresso cups and chattering of people sitting around small tables—it's exquisite. I have never experienced anything quite like it. Still a bit in awe that I've manifested an opportunity to see this man, I sit down at a caffè he recommended in the piazza to have a proper cappuccino. I send him a text message inviting him to join me for lunch. He responds, "I can't," citing house chores as a polite explanation for why, and I immediately offer an alternative, refusing to accept his response. Hopeful yet unsure about whether I have managed to sway him, I write a note in my journal.

Thank you for your generosity and kindness and thoughtfulness and chivalry. I feel safe when I'm with you. I feel taken care of. I feel loved. I feel cherished. I can feel the conflict you are in when you are with me. I don't desire that for you, but I also believe it's asking you to make a choice. I love you. I choose you. I will wait for you.

Less than an hour later, I receive a message from him telling me he can't do this. He can no longer communicate with me. And then he blocks me. I sit there, stunned and hurt. The connection I know we have was confirmed last night. We had such a lovely time. And I made it clear I am aware of his situation. I mean, am I crazy? What is happening? Why me? These thoughts race through my head. In some ways, my greatest fear has come true—again. I choose something, declare that choice, and then I lose it. Each time, I seem to get one step closer before it's taken away. Once the initial shock dissipates, I decide to do what I do when I don't understand something and need to process it. I pull out my journal once more and start a dialogue with myself.

"Well, that came out of nowhere," I begin. "I don't understand. Why did he do that?"

"Matters of the heart aren't meant to be understood. That's why they're matters of the heart, not matters of the head. There's nothing logical or rational about them. You cannot find a rational answer. So I invite you to stop trying to," my higher wisdom responds.

"I feel confused and like I don't know what I'm doing or can trust myself, and to top it off, what must others be thinking?!"

"It doesn't matter what others think. What do you know to be true? You can trust yourself. Despite what anybody else says or thinks or doesn't say."

"Can I trust myself that it is safe to choose and wait despite what he just said?"

"Yes. He is hurting right now. He is conflicted, and you knew your presence would activate something. You also knew that one of the options he has is to choose his wife and family over you."

"So then, how can I trust myself if he chooses them over me?" I wonder. "Doesn't that mean I was wrong?"

"What you feel in your heart cannot be 'wrong.' It might not unfold the way you want it to, but that doesn't make it wrong."

"So then, what does it mean if he chooses them over me?"

"Nothing. It doesn't mean anything. It's not about being chosen or not. It's about listening to and trusting yourself no matter what. Your souls called to one another," my higher wisdom assures me. "Your soul was called to him and to this place. There's no doubt about that. Now, he has the choice to do what he desires to do. That doesn't mean your soul's calling was off. I commend you for listening. Most people don't."

"He said what it looks like to him that I flew all this way—what a fool I am."

"You might feel like a fool in this precise moment, but that's not the truth of who you are. You are wise beyond your years. And it is through these experiences that you gain even more wisdom."

"What is the wisdom I am gaining here? That I can't have what I want?"

"Not at all. That you can handle whatever happens."

"But I'm tired of proving my resiliency. I know I'm resilient. I've fallen and gotten back up so many fucking times by this point. When can I finally stay upright?!"

"Simply feel it, accept it, and continue to have faith. Continue to be clear on what you desire and what you are. It will find you. I promise."

"I feel myself weary of it … yet I don't want to lose faith."

"Then, keep the faith. Deep down, you know what this is all about and why it's coming up right now."

"I do? Please elaborate."

"To show you again that you are capable and can trust yourself. Even when it's hard or doesn't seem like it. This isn't the time to give up; this is the time to lean in and stay the course. Stay committed to what you feel is true."

"That seems even more foolish."

"Bingo. That's exactly why this is coming up for you. You need to release your deep fear that committing to follow your heart is foolish. To choose something and stick with it isn't foolish; it is safe to do—even when so many things seem to tell you otherwise (mainly your own judgment and fear)."

"So, you're saying it's okay to ride this out?"

"Yes," my higher wisdom concludes, "and continue to send out love and light to him and his family. You can do this from a very non-attached, loving, clear place."

Sometimes I am in awe of what comes flowing from my fingertips. Thanks to the encouragement of my inner wisdom, I surrender once more to the reality of the situation. I know this sounds like I'm glossing over it or not acknowledging the pain I feel. It hurts. A lot. I cry. Hard. I talk with my coach, who helps me release and transmute a lot of the energy I'm feeling. But I also surrender to it. There is nothing else I can do.

The next day, after processing some of the pain and grief, I wonder if I am to stay longer or return home. I mean, I didn't come to Italy just for *him*; I came here for love. Now, it is time to prove it. What better country to fall in love with? What better country in which to fall in love with myself?! I came all this way—shouldn't I soak up all that Vicenza (and Italy) has to offer? What if there is some other reason I was guided here in the first place?

With all these questions swirling in my mind, I give space for the fear and doubts that inevitably arise. A few are primed and ready at the helm. What if I'm so consumed by love that I'm neglecting my work and business, which is where my focus ought to be? What if I go broke following my heart instead of going home and being content with what I already have? When will I learn to just be happy as I am? Without the love. Without the travel. Without the adventure. I'm so afraid that I will keep feeling disappointed and dissatisfied so long as I keep chasing after my heart's desires. Then, one of the deepest, scariest, ugliest fears I don't want to look at reared its head: What if I am meant to be content by myself and am creating unnecessary suffering by desiring a partner? Perhaps it's time to accept that I am meant to do life alone after all.

While there is some truth and wisdom to what my inner protective voice has to say, most of it is coming from a place of fear. If I've learned anything by this point in my life, I've learned to choose love over fear. So I decide to stay. I book another Airbnb, this time for a couple weeks. Even if my time here is limited, I'm certain what I receive from Italy will last a lifetime.

CHAPTER 10

FINDING UNION

Much like how, to Elizabeth Gilbert, it is the Land of Pleasure, to me, Italy is the Land of Pure, Unadulterated Acceptance. At thirty-seven and a half years old, I still find myself at times judgmental of what time I wake up or if I have one too many glasses of wine or eat a bit too much or am once again "losing myself" in the name of love. And from the moment I decide to stay, it presents me with plenty of opportunities to do just that.

Italy epitomizes "love" in every sense of the word. It seems to find me at every corner, in Venetian statues and couples kissing in the piazza and food made with love. It also appears in the form of American men, Italian men, Irish men, more Italian men, more American men .... And yet, being in Italy is like being in a classroom. Not to learn how to wake up earlier or drink less or have dessert less often or even love less deeply. Rather, it is my opportunity to love and accept myself more deeply for all these things. Here, I get to practice fully accepting myself.

I recall when my friend told me I couldn't *not* fall more in love with myself in Italy. She was right! It isn't immediate, but as I stay longer, this is exactly what happens. I start to love myself despite (and possibly because of) how long I rest, how much I enjoy the taste of wine and good food, and how deeply—and often—I fall in love, even if only for a weekend. Perhaps another day in another land, I will be asked to learn greater moderation. But after a lifetime of excessively one-sided non-acceptance and self-loathing (seems a bit harsh, but I'll go with it), I find balance by moving to the other side of that pendulum, which is excessive self-acceptance.

There is something so simple yet profound about watching a man on his way to work stop at a caffetteria to stand at the outside counter and order an espresso, have a brief chat with the barista, drink his caffè in two swallows, and then be on his way, accepting the natural flow of things. It feels so wildly different from how we go about having our coffee in the States. Gelato after lunch? How lovely. Wine with every meal? Of course. All of Italy feels classy without being pretentious, decadent without being indulgent. Even thunderstorms are more magnificent here. And people are still out and about on rooftop bars and under awnings, for the most part enjoying it. For the love of wine, it is rare to see people getting drunk. Kids in bars and dancing in the piazza at all hours of the evening—how spectacular! There is an aliveness and communal nature to this town and country.

I take long walks in the mornings, enjoying the beauty and views this city has to offer. I spend my days admiring the different shades of orange-stuccoed buildings, hearing the sounds of church bells, sitting at caffès drinking cappuccinos (before 11 a.m.) and macchiatos (past midday). Afternoons consist of a gelato break from work as I wander around the narrow, cobblestoned streets that weave through the center of town. Come evening, I sit in the piazza drinking spritz liscio (Vicenza's version of spritz bianco—just white wine and sparkling water; no Aperol for me) and eating potato chips (the standard salty snack that accompanies my aperitivo). Dinner most nights means choosing a local osteria and indulging in bigoli con l'anatra, the popular duck ragu, or gnocchi with truffle along with a glass or two of Valpolicella red wine.

Even my body adjusts to this new flow. After some initial weight gain, it seems to acclimate and even lose a few pounds. There's nothing quite like the quality of food found in other countries, especially Italy. One might think, what with all the pasta and bread and gelato consumed, getting fat is the only option. The reality, however, is that food in Italy is *real*. It is made of real ingredients and doesn't contain the sugar, chemicals, and additives like in the United States, which makes a huge difference. This, plus all the walking that comes with the lifestyle of living in an old, medium-sized Italian town (both to and from every place I patronize as well as up and down multiple flights of stairs to my apartment), keeps my body moving and feeling healthy.

Being home to multiple U.S. military bases, Vicenza is teeming with thousands of Americans, so it is very easy to meet people who speak my language (and, therefore, very difficult to learn a new one). One particular evening, a new friend of mine who works on base invites me to join him for an aperitivo. Little did I know just how important this evening would turn out to be.

Shortly after ordering our drinks, he takes note of a young woman who had approached the terrace and been seated by herself at a nearby table minutes earlier. He asks if he can invite her to join us. Of course, my answer is yes. And I'm so glad it is. Grace and I become fast friends (and the two of them become fast lovers). This evening is one of many in Italy that reminds me of my gratitude for my open heart, which brings so many meaningful connections into my life.

After a few more weeks of continuing to enjoy my daily routine, deepen connections with my new friends, and work with clients from across the world, it is time to venture out and visit a few other places, first by myself, then with the friends I have met. I take a short trip to Bologna, a nearby city that a few people have now recommended I check out. It is bigger than Vicenza and known as the Italian equivalent of a "college town," given it is home to a large university and filled with young people from all around the country (and perhaps even the world).

On one of my solo evenings there (after getting one of the best haircuts of my life), I wander through the porticoes and streets, crowded with people eating, drinking, and laughing beneath buildings that were built nearly one thousand years ago. I feel aware of the duality— and oneness—of life. I can feel lonely amidst all this companionship surrounding me. I can feel sad while they exude joy and laughter. I can feel lost while they know exactly where they are. I can get turned away from a restaurant while it is full of others enjoying the food. A question comes to mind as I meander around, feeling lost and a bit forlorn: What am I looking for?

Without much further thought, I remember my answer. I am looking for union. Yes, within myself. But *also* with another. I desire partnership. I want to explore the streets hand-in-hand. I want to see the sculptures while my beloved's arm is around me. I desire to sit in a caffè with someone and spend time together. I want to have another to whom I can give my love (and receive his in return). I long to be witnessed and observed from without as much as from within.

A life unexamined (or perhaps better to say "unwitnessed") seems pointless. Here I am, enjoying some of the most beautiful parts of the world, enjoying delicious food and wine, seeing gorgeous sites all around me, having ideas and observations about love, life, and the universe, and there is no one to share it all with, no one to witness it with me (and me with it). This is a very familiar feeling. I remember when I traveled in Europe for the first time nearly seven years ago, alone with very similar sensations and thoughts. Thing is, that's all they are. Thoughts and feelings. They are not who I am. I know this. And these thoughts and feelings can follow me anywhere in the world.

One evening, I am sitting on a patio sipping a glass of rosé and reading *The Course of Love*, lent to me by my newfound friend Grace, whose appreciation for words and big ideas was a point of immediate connection between us. I receive some clarity about why I am such a romantic. It is my way of making sense of this thing called life. This existential dilemma each of us faces. This Lila. We are all seeking meaning in life. Some of us do it by having children or making a lot of money or building a business; some of us do it by traveling to faraway lands or falling in love (some of us try to do all of that at the same time!). Instead of seeking God or status (which I have also had my fair share of), at this stage of my life, I seek love.

I have spent the last few years worried that I don't know how to attract and hold onto the partner I want. I seem to push it away or kill it before it even begins. Or so I've told myself. Relationships seem to be the thing I've been addicted and attached to most of all in my life, starting with me staying in relationships long after their expiration date and then spending countless hours contemplating how to become someone better fit for partnership, how to attract the perfect man, how to find the love I seek.

Love and partnership have consumed much of my thoughts, conversations, contemplations, and experiences for years now. Some people struggle with alcoholism; some with disordered eating; I struggle with trying to make sense of relationships. This seems to be my "cross to bear." While not a victim, I am here to work with and heal and integrate my experience of attachment and feeling I need to be a certain way to have the relationship I want. Yes, I wish I didn't show up the way I sometimes (okay, most times) do at the initial stage of romantic relationships. This is when I feel least secure and most anxious. This is when it seems like I have no control over how often I message or what I say. This is when I feel the most amount of discomfort and believe the only way to relieve it is by saying more, not less. The same part of me that's willing to take a leap and reach out to my beloved is sometimes the part that seems to cause him to back away. Equally, until I accept myself for who I am and how I show up, I will continue to attract those into my life who also aren't okay with it.

What would it look like for me to fully accept this about myself? Much like an alcoholic must first admit he has a problem and needs help from a Higher Power, what if that Higher Power is radical self-acceptance and love for how I am showing up? I can always make a new choice if I desire to and, equally, when I don't make a new choice and still operate from this place of insecurity and fear, that's also okay. It's only through acceptance that I can set my cross down and experience more of my authentic power. When my personality and soul are aligned, there's acceptance that this is "who I am." This is the sort of union I desire within myself. And I am getting a taste of it here.

And yet, even in this country where I feel greater self-acceptance and self-love than ever before, I find myself stuck on the same old question: So, why travel, then? If I can come to terms with the fact that I can feel sad and lonely from anywhere, why not just stay in Sioux Falls? Well, I would counter that with, why *not* go somewhere else? There may have been a time when I traveled because I wanted to experience something grand or prove something or not feel stuck. But now? I travel because I enjoy it. I enjoy putting myself in situations that are uncomfortable and out of my familiarity zone. When I travel, I reinforce the knowing that I am always supported and cared for. I am constantly reminded of how similar we all are despite our unique differences. I am reminded how connected I am to everyone and all that is. I get to experience the truth of who I am amidst the duality and the joy.

Perhaps life isn't about "finding what we're looking for" but rather coming to terms with the fact that we will find whatever it is wherever we are and that the thing we are searching for is not found in an external location. Yes, I realize this is not a unique realization, but it finally clicks. No matter where we are, we will have a similar experience because there is no such thing as escaping the human experience.

Travel, for me, is synonymous with following my heart—*following*, after so many years of what has felt like chasing. It is a vulnerable act, allowing for the flow of life. Taking a trip is a leap of faith. Vulnerability and surrender go hand in hand. We often don't surrender (or allow ourselves to be supported) because it feels vulnerable to do so. It can be difficult to experience this from the comfort of our homes or what we already know to be familiar and secure. When "forced" outside of our comfort zones, we open ourselves up to more experiences and opportunities to feel this level of support.

With even more self-awareness and self-love, I head to Florence, where Grace will meet me. Arriving there, I now understand what that British woman was talking about in my favorite coffee shop back home. This city is beyond breathtaking. The duomo looks fake, it is so beautiful. Thanks to my worldly friend, I get to visit some of the best restaurants and wine bars—she has a knack for finding the hidden gems of a place. After spending a couple of days walking along the Arno and seeing many statues of David (most of them, I learn, are actually fake) and eating incredible Florentine food, we take a train to Rome where I see even more beautiful structures and eat fresh mozzarella with my bare hands before making our way back up to Vicenza via Pisa and Cinque Terre.

Returning to Vicenza after my short tour around other Italian cities feels like coming home. One evening, enjoying a glass of Prosecco with Grace, I say, "I'm home. I want to move here." I've been in Italy for nearly a month, and for the first time since I had left San Francisco three years prior, I am ready to choose. I am beginning to realize that any choice is okay. It's making the choice that matters (which is the only "control" I have), and I choose Vicenza.

Even for how amazing my time in Costa Rica was and how much that place also felt like home, there is something about Italy. This country feels more secure and stable (not just the internet, though that is a major stability feature). As exotic and magical as Costa Rica is, I feel ready for something that can provide for me. This experience has clearly shown me what I currently desire in my life. If Costa Rica is the attractive, laidback, shiny object that sounds like a whole lot of fun (and, trust me, it is!), then Italy is the stable, secure, intuitively known connection. If Costa Rica is the hot surfer dude, Italy is the reliable man you take home to your parents.

The next day, I give notice to my property manager (for the second time in less than a year) and book a ticket back to Sioux Falls. By the end of the following week, I am ready to vacate my small apartment, my anchor point for nearly a year.

Once again, I get rid of most of my belongings. Each time I move, I let go of more and more things that metaphorically and literally weigh me down, and by this point, there isn't much left. Still, this move invites me to release even more of what I have been carrying around for nearly two decades—boxes of yearbooks, childhood journals, love letters, photos (including from my wedding). I go through each box, sitting with the various notes and memories, letting emotions come and go. I no longer need a book or picture or piece of writing to remind me who I am. I no longer need these memorabilia to prove or validate my existence. I am no longer the person who wrote these journal entries or received these letters or was in these photos. All of this has influenced and become part of who I am, but it isn't who I am. Who I am is not found in those boxes. After taking a picture or two of what I want to cherish a bit more (mainly the love letters that date back to when I was fifteen years old), I carry the boxes to the dumpster and throw them away. The remaining items fit into the three boxes that I will ship to Vicenza. The rest I will pack into two suitcases and carry with me.

The time has come for me to say goodbye to Sioux Falls (for real this time). As I stand in the doorway of my empty studio apartment, I give gratitude for these 450 square feet that have served as my place to land for the past year and expanded me in so many ways. I am not the same woman I was when I arrived. Ready and eager to call Italy home, I place the key on the counter and close the door behind me without looking back, feeling simultaneously confident and uncertain about my decision and what lies ahead.

CHAPTER 11

KEEPING THE FAITH

It seems I was just packing for my move to Italy when I once again find myself gathering up what I've selected to see me through my next chapter. Folding my favorite new dress from the local market, I reflect on my time since leaving Sioux Falls for good as I prepare to head to the airport and board my flight to Marco Polo once again. I have spent most of September in Costa Rica, enjoying what this country offers me and now ready to return to my more solid choice. It's been an enriching month of working with the client I was introduced to through the woman I met at Sound & Silence and hosting my first writer's retreat (also inspired by that previous trip here). The retreat was beyond transformative for everyone, myself included.

About five months ago, when I received the nudge to host it here, I felt scared and vulnerable. Who am I to lead a retreat? Who would say yes to that? With the support of my coach, I allowed my fear to turn into excitement, but it felt like such a big leap of faith, financially and emotionally. But, step by step, I trusted and followed the guidance I received. Each time, instead of turning away, I faced my fears and discomforts, including those around setting a price for participants, not making enough to cover the costs, or feeling rejected. I reached out to dozens of people directly, sharing with them my vision and the invitation to join me. In return, I received confirmation after confirmation that the individuals I felt compelled to reach out to, more often than not, experienced a sense of synchronicity in my timing. Some of them said "no," some said "maybe," and more than a dozen said "YES!!!" As I have learned, I don't get to control the outcome or other people.

Equally, there were moments that briefly challenged my courage and confidence, such as when someone let me know she couldn't make it after all and requested a refund of her money. Instead of wavering and falling out of integrity with what I had already established as my "terms," I found the courage to release her gracefully and offer her an opportunity to apply the money toward a future opportunity together. A couple of other people backed out, but I held my ground and was fully supported.

Days before the retreat began, a few more pieces shifted, but instead of worrying or fretting or getting upset, I trusted the process and the unfolding and was guided to exactly the right people to support me with what I needed. I stretched wider and wider, a few small things tested my edges, yet I maintained my trust that all would be well—and it was! Entering into the retreat, I felt so supported, guided, and confident. In fact, the most discomfort I felt leading up to it was due to my *lack* of stress and worry.

The retreat opened with thirteen of us gathering together for a sacred cacao ceremony. It was beyond what anyone—even I—had expected. Everyone immediately connected on various levels. Other than a few feeling weary from travel, the energy felt so good. The next five days together revealed miracle after miracle and synchronicity after synchronicity. The facilitators, who include Rodolfo as well as other space holders and healers who showed up (some only days before the retreat was scheduled to start), were incredible. The container felt so strong and safe and held. And I felt I could relax and allow for others to take the lead whenever needed.

Others reflected back to me how wonderful it was to witness me create such a collaborative space and show a new way for holding retreats that isn't all about me as the main attraction or controlling each and every thing. I had no idea at the get-go that this is the sort of experience I would create, though I'm not surprised, as that is how I prefer to show up in the world. It is so powerful to witness myself in others as they step into the spotlight and share their gifts, which so divinely mirror or complement mine.

The week felt easeful and spacious. Everything from the space to the food to the workshops to the "free time" to the conversations to the individual personalities who showed up was beyond divine and anything I could have hoped or planned for. Even in moments of emotion and trigger, the group remained cohesive. I found myself able to allow each person to have her or his experience without needing to fix it or even change it or feel I needed to do anything more. Only once or twice did I observe the old me show up and feel like maybe she wasn't "doing enough," but that quickly subsided as I acknowledged the fear or shared it with someone who reflected back to me my truth.

I was seen as the mother of the group, which was so warming to my heart. I witnessed incredible transformation occur with each and every participant. Daily, I was filled with awe and gratitude that this is the experience I've been called to co-create. This is how it feels to be a channel for source energy to live through me. It was very evident to me that this didn't happen "by" me but rather "through" me. And this is when true transformation and value can be offered to others. Had I tried to plan or control this, I know beyond a shadow of a doubt it would not have been as magical as it was—for me and for each person there.

If my retreat in Costa Rica was an exercise in seeing there is less I need to "do" or "control," then moving to Italy is a chance to continue knowing I am always supported by Infinite Spirit, limitlessly and imme-diately. Entrepreneurship is not for the faint of heart. "Lucky" for me, I have had many opportunities to cultivate inner security as I've been without the security of consistent money. Not that there's anything wrong with money—it can be great, and it's super useful. I simply see how I have a relationship with it that is not based in our traditional capitalistic ways. As such, I do not feel the need to exert control over money, which includes feeling the need to accumulate or manage it. After all, I have plenty of other things I try to exert control over.

My fears (of money, of scarcity and loss) seem to be left behind as I arrive back in Vicenza, still uncertain what I will do three months from now when I will need to reset my tourist visa. Yet I am calm. If only I could transfer this same philosophy to love ....

As it was over a month ago, Italy continues to be a classroom for me. These months bring with them continued growth and expansion in my business along with some very dark moments. At times, it isn't very comfortable. Other times, it is downright painful. The land of pleasure is also, at times, the land of pain, and I am reminded of that poignant duality I experienced here months earlier.

There are two sides to every experience. The gift is found when we can feel and realize them occurring simultaneously. When we can feel the pain in the pleasure and the pleasure in the pain—you know, when something "hurts so good" or when you "laugh until you cry." Despite all the pleasure I experience, for many weeks, I find myself feeling very depressed.

The months of November and December mark the depths of this darkness. I feel aimless. I cry a lot. I lose touch with my "why." I feel so confused. Why have I come all this way and still feel like I haven't gotten very far? Why am I still struggling with the same things I always struggle with? I feel once again that I am being blocked from receiving what I want, whether it is a simple object like a podcast mic or a yoni egg or the man I deeply love who still lives in Vicenza. When I am able to have a sense of humor about it, it really can be quite ridiculous how the universe has me work this edge of mine.

The yoni egg, I order for a virtual workshop I am attending. I'm relieved to be in a place where postal delivery is more reliable than I've heard it is in Costa Rica, and the recommended seller of this item "just so happens" to be based in Italy—what are the odds? I place my order and am told it will take a few days to arrive from a few towns away. I track the shipment for the entire estimated delivery period, and the parcel still shows it hasn't been mailed. My workshop has started by now, yet I keep the faith and continue to track the package through my confusion.

Finally, the package is "en route" and should arrive any day. I go to the maildrop location and am informed there is no package for me. I wait another day and check the status again to see that it has been returned to its origin. What?! By this point, we are well into the workshop, and I am quite frustrated. The whole point is to have this egg. Why am I not receiving it?

As I'm learning the level of patience and surrender demanded of courier services in Italy, I order a podcast mic. This time, I use an international shipping company—what could go wrong? Within a week or two, my podcast would be up and running from Italy. Well, for whatever reason, this package is also delayed. My intention to continue sharing my journey with the world using a decent microphone seems to be off the table for the foreseeable future.

In each scenario, I try everything I know how to do to receive something, and still it's not here. Waiting for a package to be delivered, I'm afraid that if I don't check the status of the shipment daily, it will never arrive. Waiting for love, I'm afraid that if I don't keep going out and meeting other men, I will be alone for the rest of my life. I want to feel like I'm at least doing something while I sit by and wait. As uncomfortable as it can be, the universe seems to be actively reminding me that sometimes all I can do is be patient. The rest is not within my control. These lessons are bringing me into a deeper sense of surrender, which brings up all the feelings: sadness, anger, frustration, blame, guilt, vulnerability, acceptance. Being blocked from receiving these objects feels familiar to having been blocked a few months back by my deeper desire, the man who cut off communication.

A few weeks after the shipping debacles, while talking about relationships with a friend over dinner, I find myself unable to answer a simple question of his: "What makes you happy?" I respond defensively, holding very tightly to certain thought forms. "Nothing 'makes' me feel anything," I say. Sneaky part is, these thought forms seem to be "right" and "spiritual"—such as how I am not a victim and things can't "make" me feel a certain way, which I start to notice is something I find unacceptable. When I explore my strong reaction, I find

I am afraid that if I admit that circumstances or people "make" me feel a certain way, then I am considering myself a victim and will lose myself and all that I have worked toward. I would be admitting that something outside me can control my experience of life and that I am affected by others. The wonderful thing about this realization is that it's not true. I am affected by others, but they do not control my life or make me a victim. It is yet another reminder that I can never lose who I am because who I am is far beyond any of these thoughts and beliefs. I'm beginning to see it's safe to be affected by life and other people—including courier services.

Being human includes having emotions and feelings that arise, at times, "without choice." This does not mean I am a victim; it simply means I am experiencing the full breadth of being human. I am embracing all of it, which, paradoxically, is true non-attachment. It is remaining free despite whatever is happening "to" me or "limiting" me. As vulnerable as it is to not be in control, there is freedom in looking to others to provide me with something—*if* and when I hold all of it lightly.

This same friend of mine helps me see more clearly the other unconscious belief that is operating. If I fear I can be victimized and controlled by others, that also means I fear I can be the perpetrator and control others—they go hand-in-hand (along with believing I can save someone, like Michael, for example). For this very reason, much like I have been afraid to speak my truth, I am also uncomfortable asking for what I want from others because I'm afraid I'm controlling them by doing so.

I have thought for a long time that the hesitation to express my desires stems from the fear of being disappointed when they don't come true (and, therefore, that I am a "victim" of my circumstances). But I'm beginning to see how this has been a cover-up for my deeper fear that if I clearly express my desires, I'm manipulating or controlling another. Funny how I didn't have that fear when it came to clearly expressing to the universe the sort of apartment I wanted. Apparently, it's not as easy for me to do when speaking directly to another person. But when I don't express my desires clearly, it can lead to confusion for the one helping me realize my dreams and desires—the masculine principle, often meaning the partner I am calling in.

Similarly, it occurs to me that I am unconsciously avoiding partnership because I fear being disappointed. One of my greatest fears of a true love story might be that it actually won't "solve anything" and, worse yet, that it might be so disappointing that I'll actually feel worse off. That it won't magically deliver me from my pain or angst or disappointment or feelings of loneliness. That a partnership won't be my "savior" (see how insidious this whole victim triangle thing is?).

With all that I'm experiencing (and all the ways the universe is showing up to "help"), what I'm willing to accept more fully than ever before is that disappointment is a part of life (and that doesn't make me a victim). I am having this lightbulb moment—what if this unconscious (or maybe very conscious) desire that being in a relationship will relieve me of what it means to experience the human condition is what has kept me from being in a relationship? Because it absolutely won't do that. Nothing is intended to do that. I'm not here to free myself from being human; I'm here to free myself from anything keeping me from being *more* of my whole self, which includes this human experience I have chosen.

Taking my morning walk the next day, I think about how Italy, to me, represents finding freedom within the human condition as opposed to trying to escape it, which I feel so many of us try to do. Sometimes being human sucks. Sometimes it hurts. I see why so many philosophies and religions talk about denying oneself desire and pleasure—if there's no desire, no longing, and no pleasure, there is no pain (or so we think). But why is pain such a dirty word? Why is pain something to avoid? If pain is to be avoided, then pleasure is to be avoided. And why avoid pleasure? To avoid pain? What a vicious cycle. But, again, resisting one side of things would be resisting my full self and trying to control the human condition, to free myself from pain. And that's not what I'm here to free myself from.

What if I am more afraid of being in partnership than single for this very reason—the pain it will cause? I stop in my tracks as it hits me. There is no one thing or person who will meet all my wants, needs, and desires all of the time. There is no one thing or person who will last forever. All I've been doing is trying to protect myself from the inevitable heartbreak I will experience when what I love with all my being lets me down or is gone.

And here's the sneakiest, most upsetting part of it all: the knowing that ultimately I *will* "lose" everything, no matter what I do (right, wrong, good, bad, a product of control or surrender), is what it means to be human and have this impermanent experience. No matter what we do in order to keep this from being true, it is. This body will die. This experience will end. This person will leave or die. This relationship, in its current state, will expire and transform. This baby will turn into a child and into an adult. This parent will no longer be around to talk to. Loss, or rather the feeling of loss, is a certainty.

It's okay to be upset or angry about this. It is understandable as a human to feel this emotion because it doesn't "make sense." We are programmed to believe that if we "do things the right way, the appropriate way, the ideal way, the moral way," we'll avoid heartache and pain, become immortal, and get it all. The harder thing to accept is that it doesn't ultimately matter. At the end of the day, we all know how this story ends. It ends in "loss." And that *is* something to be angry about. At least for a time. Allowing this, accepting this, acknowledging this feels like a lump in my throat and a pit in my stomach. Once it is painfully (or joyously) clear that there is nothing I can or cannot do (nothing to control or manipulate and nothing to be a victim of) when it comes to keeping or losing something, I am truly free to embrace all of it, feel all of it, experience all of it, and drop the defenses. I am free to be all of who I am.

In a way, I've chosen this life for the freedom it offers me. But, I'm beginning to wonder, is it truly freedom? Because every coin has two sides. I have chosen to live where I live and do what I do even though I know it might keep me from feeling secure and stable in my life. Being single also keeps me from feeling secure and stable in my life. Of course, it also feels less risky than letting someone see my insecurities up close and personal or feeling the full spectrum of human emotion, which can feel destabilizing. Interesting how, no matter what, there is an experience of instability. But perhaps, rather than an opportunity for blame and shame and guilt and all that, this is the opportunity and invitation to accept it.

This brings me back to how security, like freedom, is an inside job. It is time to experience less external freedom (being "free as a bird") and practice experiencing more internal freedom (feeling secure in who I am, no matter the circumstances). This free bird is looking for a cage, in a sense. The cage isn't necessarily a person or a place; it's found in me knowing without a doubt I can follow my heart (free from care or concern). It's a sense of security so that I can be free to follow my soul's desires (this is the paradox of life).

On December 31, just hours before the year and decade come to completion, I sit in my cozy apartment overlooking the piazza below, reflecting on the year and decade soon to pass. These past ten years have taught me my worth and abundance, starting with my corporate job in 2010. Since then, I have found my dharma and learned how to listen to my soul. I have learned self-love and compassion on a whole new level. I have written a book. I have moved eight times, each time learning more about letting go. I have practiced faith and trusting my intuition more than ever before. I have fallen in love many times and had my heart broken just as many. I have prepared myself for my life partner and what is to come.

At this point in my life, I desire partnership in order to experience the fullness and breadth of the human condition. It won't relieve me of having a human experience; it will ask me to show up even more fully in my humanness (and let that be intimately seen by another). I don't desire a man to remove me from the feelings of being human—I want to drop into them more deeply and truly. I'll still feel grief and loneliness in addition to joy and gratitude, all while being witnessed by another. Am I ready for that again? Am I ready for someone else to see me in my fullness? Am I ready for someone to see my uncertainty, my fear, my insecurity so up close and personal, knowing what I now know? I desire to keep my heart open, trusting and softening into this, which feels super vulnerable and requires me letting go of certainty and control (in the way I often think of it).

I give tremendous gratitude for 2019. Many times over the course of the year, I have seen how I hold onto a story that I can't trust myself or relax when, in reality, that isn't at all true. Why have I held onto it, then? To unconsciously keep myself from desiring what I desire because the fear is greater—I will eventually lose it and myself in the process. I've learned more and more that it is okay to desire someone and things to "make me happy." I can be impacted by desires without being a victim. It is okay and safe to be human.

So, why not passionately declare my wants? What if there is no doubt in my mind that this is coming to me as strongly as I believe that I'm always supported and cared for? Can I be clear on what I desire without attaching to or trying to control the outcome?

Before ringing in the new decade, I finally allow myself to reclaim and recommit to my knowing that, all along, it has been the man I met on Father's Day. Once more, I open myself to that possibility and choose him, still with no certainty that I will ever hear from him again. Am I willing to let my heart hold what I know to be true while letting go of control?

When I accept that I have already found him, the part of me seeking love can rest. The part of me that clings to searching must die and be reborn, reintegrated into the larger, all-having self. I die to the belief that I am still searching for him. I die to the idea that I have any control over the matter (if he ever comes back, it will be up to him, not me). And my fear of committing to my soul's knowing can "die," giving me the strength and courage to move forward with confidence that everything I desire is on its way to me, and all I have to do is be patient. There is a grieving process for this necessary loss. And this loss is necessary for the next version of self to emerge. Once something is found, something is lost, and freedom is gained. The freedom here is rooted in a deep commitment to love, not a running away or being detached from it.

For all that I have "lost," I have found so many other things in Italy. I have found Grace (literally and metaphorically). I have found how to enjoy the pleasures of life again. I have found greater trust, love, and acceptance for myself. I have found my humanity. I have found how to keep coming back to my belief, my knowing, my willingness to control the things I can (my attitude, my beliefs, my thoughts, my actions, my focus) and then release the rest (including my judgment about control), trusting and knowing it is all working out divinely.

I can't rush nature. Everything has its own time. I don't get to control when or how it happens, even if I know it will. Just like there are cycles and patterns to nature and we know certain things will happen (the sun will set, the moon will rise, the flowers will bloom, the leaves will fall), we don't control them. How many times have I tried to pry the bloom open before it is ready? How many times have I wanted to give up because it hasn't yet happened? Equally, how many times have I returned to a deeper, stiller knowing and practiced patience? How many times have I trusted it will happen, and then it does?

For 2020, my word is "confidence." I welcome the year with firm trust and certainty. I love the layers of meaning here. Confidence in myself, confidence in the universe, confidence in others, confidence that all is coming in perfect divine time (which implies patience). I enter this new decade certain of my worth and desires, trusting myself, having compassion for myself and others, doing what I love, and ready to be with my beloved and start a family together whenever that time comes. As I now more deeply accept, there is a greater timing to it all. Others play a part, with their own levels of responsibility, and the waiting might be uncomfortable. But it will end—everything does. And eventually, everything I've wanted—the mic, the yoni egg, and the man—will find their way to me.

CHAPTER 12

WAITING IT OUT

Leaving Vicenza brings up more emotion than I expect. As I walk around town one crisp winter day, saying goodbye to my new friends and favorite caffè owners, baristas, and bartenders, I pause to stand on the steps of Palladio's Basilica and sob. I don't understand why—I am leaving my things with a friend and coming back in three months. It's just a visa run, and I'll visit some friends and family, go to a wedding (Daniel became someone else's "Mr. Right"), and host another retreat in Costa Rica. I'll be back by April.

It is January 2020, and the U.S. I return to from Europe is different from how I remember. Traveling through airports and going out with friends, I notice that things seem a bit off, but I don't make much of it. I'm more aware of something being a bit "off" internally—in a good way. I am no longer "searching for him," having made such a clear declaration and decision within myself that I have already found him. The search is over. I can finally rest and relax. For so many years, my default setting has been to be on the lookout for whenever I might meet the man I would spend my life with. It hasn't always been a conscious thing, but I sure notice when I am no longer doing it. It catches me by surprise, but it's a very nice surprise. I navigate the world from a new perspective, moving around more confidently and less distractedly. It is a big energetic shift.

But that isn't all that's changed. By the time I arrive in Los Angeles in February for the wedding, I am increasingly aware of strange things happening around me—and I'm not talking about miraculous synchronicities or metaphysical experiences, which are far from strange in my world. Friends begin to update me on what is happening (for years now, I have made it a point not to follow the news), and by this point, the fear and mandates are making their way to the West Coast, where I am. I begin to feel the impact.

I have already scheduled a flight to Costa Rica for the third week of March, where I plan to stay for a few weeks to host my second writer's retreat and work with my client there before returning to Vicenza. By the second week of March, there is talk of borders closing. I am in disbelief. Countries aren't actually going to start closing borders because of some virus, are they? I, for one, am certainly not going to let fear start making my decisions again.

Six days before I am scheduled to depart LAX, an inner voice says, "Get on an earlier flight." I dismiss it at first, thinking it might simply be fear speaking—after all, there was a lot of it going around. I push the voice away. The next day, it returns louder. "Go to the airport and get on an earlier flight." *Fine, okay.* This time, I trust it is my intuition, not fear, speaking to me. After all, this isn't the first time my inner guidance has told me to go to the airport and been onto something. I get in my rental car and drive down the 110.

After speaking with the agent at the counter for about twenty minutes, I have a ticket scheduled for that night. Somehow, I'm not charged an extra penny for it. When I board the plane, I have an entire row to myself for the five-hour red-eye. Landing in the Costa Rican capital of San José early Sunday morning, I grab a coffee at the Juan Santamaría Airport while I sort out my next step. Since I've arrived a few days earlier than planned, I don't have anything lined up yet. I find a nearby resort hotel on the spot and book it for free with points. Not too shabby for traveling without any plans (as a true traveler does).

From the moment I step off the plane, I feel peace wash over my body. There is just something about Costa Rica. Each time I arrive here, I feel a comfort of home, much like Italy, while simultaneously very different. As I arrive at the hotel, walking through the lobby on my way to the front desk, I read the ticker tape on the news channel announcing that the president of Costa Rica is closing the borders on Wednesday. My original flight had been scheduled to arrive Thursday. Huh. I am instantly grateful I listened to my intuition. I can't imagine being stuck in L.A., unable to get here and potentially not be able to leave the U.S. until who knows when. With everything going on in the world, I decide to cancel my upcoming retreat, but I still have a client and friends to visit, thanks to my previous trips here. Plus, I have another few weeks before I am scheduled to return to Italy, so I embrace the border closures as a sign I'm meant to stay.

I immediately sink back into the feeling of being here, surrounded by the sounds of birds, waves, dogs, bugs buzzing in my ear as I sleep. This country forces me into greater silence and listening, sometimes with no cell service and often limited WiFi. There's a natural rhythm of things. The town seems to wake up and come alive as the sun rises and goes to bed when it sets, which is on a perfectly balanced twelve-hour cycle. I love how things seem to flow together here—cars, bikes, pedestrians, mopeds, tuk-tuks. This is the way of things, and it brings me back to my own nature, my own flow. I watch the people around me and think, "There's such simplicity and devotion and meditation and yoga in each day here. Wouldn't we all be so lucky."

I enjoy this simpler way of being. Being in a third-world country reminds me that we don't actually need much as humans. I notice how often the people here smile and wonder, do they naturally smile more? Do they have fewer worries? It reminds me of the Tao—the more we consume in the mind (and there is *so much* to consume, especially in first-world countries), the dirtier the window gets and the more often we need to clean it. Equally, something like trying to get a package delivered can be even more complex than in Italy—we know how much I loved that process.

Just like with life, with complexity often comes simultaneous simplicity. Simple in that everything is interconnected and interdependent;

complex in that everything is interconnected and interdependent. Costa Rica, like nature, is a great teacher in these matters. Simplicity is not found (or lost, for that matter) in the external world but rather in one's state of mind.

From time to time, I hear what's going on in other parts of the world—the United States and Italy, specifically. Lockdowns, mandates, people not leaving their houses. The various travel restrictions continue, and my one month here turns into two. Then, two turn into six. The Costa Rican government announces they will extend tourist visas until June of 2021, and just like that, I have been gifted an opportunity to stay without needing to leave the country for any reason for nearly another year.

What I am experiencing here is very different from what I hear from other places. My time is spent gathering with friends, moving freely about the country, going out, enjoying life. Sure, for a period of time, we have to wear masks in grocery stores, and there are some driving restrictions and curfews. But, compared to much of the world, I recognize I am still experiencing immense freedom. Every day, I am grateful for where I am.

I am also a little confused. I actively chose Italy over Costa Rica and have been clear on what I want, yet what I want isn't available to me now or for the foreseeable future. After all my work to choose where I would call home, why did I end up here? This isn't what I chose. But I still have a choice: I get to choose how I respond to what is happening. I get to choose if I resist or accept the fact that I am "stuck" in Costa Rica while the world is on global lockdown. Who knows when the world is going to open up again? I'm certainly not in control of that. And I'm not about to travel until I can do so freely (without mandates controlling where I can or cannot go). Yet I trust I am exactly where I am supposed to be, doing exactly what I am meant to be doing. So, I decide to accept my reality, to wait and see.

When I say "wait," that doesn't mean to stop living. "Waiting" is not always what we think it is—putting our life on hold for something, twiddling our thumbs, holding our breath, feeling anxious each and every day until something happens. It means accepting and surrendering to what is while acknowledging that something will change in the future, as everything eventually does. It simply means to "stay where one is or delay action," which doesn't mean *never* taking action again but rather *postponing* action. In the case of my home, I am not going to take action to leave or travel *right now*. In the case of my beloved, I am not going to actively search for someone. I'm not writing off travel ever again or telling myself I will live in Costa Rica for the rest of my life, just as I'm not writing off my beloved or telling myself I will be single the rest of my life. When I "wait" for life to lead me where I'm meant to go, it doesn't mean I don't get to have desires. I have desires, and these desires keep me opening my heart again and again, which guides me to what I want.

I start to realize that the only reason I keep feeling I need to search for or "create" what I want as opposed to sitting back and allowing it to come to me is because waiting requires even greater trust and surrender. It means I must realize that my desires have been clearly heard and received and are on their way to me. If I simply sit back and wait, then it might appear like I don't have to "do" anything to receive exactly what my soul desires. Now, this doesn't mean I don't take action, which is the tricky part about this whole thing and what I'm learning to discern from this new perspective. And yet, the primary *doing* is knowing and expressing my true desires, knowing I am completely worthy and deserving to receive them, and then embodying that truth, which is a state of *being*. I need not prove anything to receive all I desire. Yet having spent most of my life operating from an imbalance of masculine or yang energy (as many of us do, given this is the predominant energy of our modern-day society), this has been a big learning curve for me.

"Waiting it out" comes with plenty of challenges and lessons to learn. I seem to find those wherever I go (wherever I go, there I am.) One of the hardest things about waiting is how often I can find myself feeling insecure or unworthy. Thankfully, over the years, most of the thoughts that used to predominately fill my mind about doing something wrong are quieter and more distant. But I still allow myself to believe from time to time that perhaps I'm just not meant to get what I want, which makes waiting for the inevitable letdown even harder. For as much practice as I am getting, patience and delaying things aren't my strong suit.

I am not looking for him when I meet a new Daniel on the Full Moon in May. I've been in Costa Rica for a few months now, enjoying the relatively new experience of letting things take the time they take. It certainly isn't the first time I've encountered a man at an auspicious time of the month when desires are coming to their fruition (I guess this is kind of my thing), and we have an immediate connection (of course). By June, we move in together, and yet again I am certain I have met my person.

I realize I committed to the man in Italy just last New Year's, yet I still have no idea if I will ever hear from him again. I have also committed to following my heart in each moment. And now, I have been delivered someone in the flesh who is available and also embodies the qualities I wrote about more than a year ago.

There's a lot I can say about this deep and meaningful relationship. With this Daniel, my love finds a place to flow. I am excited that my dreams could be coming to fruition in a completely unexpected way. Our relationship is intense (we both have suns in Pisces, after all). We are the physical embodiment of the yin and the yang. Shortly after meeting, we even talk about having a child. We start a podcast, hiring a videographer to capture our life, and facilitate workshops about conscious relationships and embodied expression. We reflect back to each other our deepest fears and desires, just as Ram Dass says about our mirrors—that's what a guru is. If being with my ex, Michael, meant that more of my shadow qualities were reflected back to me in order to love and embrace, with Daniel, more of my light is reflected back to me for the same reasons. My spiritual gifts are further activated and heightened with this man, as are his with me.

Equally, this level of activation and intensity isn't always easy. Being this close to our mirror can be super triggering. Daniel and I move from place to place due to availability and finding the best solution to remain near his son. Despite the beautiful spaces we find together, including the entirely glass house we've been living in, complete with a small pool overlooking a valley, all of the moving around starts to take a toll. Our current rental is soon to be unavailable and, as in years past, I'm unsure what exactly will come next.

In addition, Daniel recently started taking a lot of space from me and "keeping his energy clean," which meant not even hugging me. I was starting to feel unwanted and unimportant (a major wound of mine), especially when he'd then spend time and share intimacy with other people more than me. Per usual, when I am feeling all the feelings, I write out a dialogue with myself to see what wants to be revealed.

"What desires to be expressed and heard and acknowledged right now?" I ask.

"Me! I do."

"And you are … ?"

"Your sadness, your grief, your emotions. I desire to be heard and seen and acknowledged. I simply want to be felt. I want to be given a seat at the table."

"Okay. I'm listening, and I hear you and see you. What are you feeling in this moment? What desires to be expressed now?"

"I am tired of defending myself. I am tired of proving I deserve to be here," this part of me explains.

Wow, that sounds awfully familiar. That feels like something I've realized for myself in other ways ….

"What are you defending?" I continue.

"My right to exist. My right to be here. My right to receive."

"Let's go back to your right to exist. What does it mean to defend one's right to exist?"

"I feel I have to defend my reason for existence. I have to prove I'm worthy and valuable. I have to defend why I'm here."

"And if you don't?"

"Then, I'm afraid I will die. I'm afraid I will no longer matter. I'm afraid …"

"Go on. What are you afraid of if you don't defend your existence?"

"If I don't defend my existence, I don't know why I'm here. I'll exist just because I exist. If I don't know why I'm here, I feel useless, purposeless. I mean, what's the point, then? Of being here?"

"Ah, okay. So, in order to have a point to be here, you create one (or many) and then defend it?"

"Yes. And in defending it, I forget myself."

"Now, how do desires and letting life come to you have to do with all this?"

"When I'm busy defending my reason for existing, for being here, I feel like it's up to me to put things in motion; it's up to me to create signs and synchronicities and pathways; it's up to me to keep moving."

"And is there something here about constantly feeling the need to create a reason to keep moving, to not 'land'?" I gently inquire.

"If I don't allow myself to 'land,' I get to keep believing I'm unwanted or 'don't belong anywhere,' which creates a reason for me to defend my being here. Vicious cycle. Because if I actually believe I'm wanted and belong exactly where I am, then I would simply *be* there. I would simply *arrive*. I would enjoy being. I would no longer struggle or battle with myself that it's time to move on—that I've 'overstayed my welcome.' I wouldn't keep telling myself that I need to 'find where I belong' before I can relax. I would simply relax right here, where I am right now. I would trust that I'm exactly where I am meant to or need to be in this exact moment, at all times. And I would no longer need to believe that I have to prove anything to anyone."

This is such a strong pattern in my life—feeling I don't belong, needing to prove and defend myself. Not only in the way I feel, but my existence as a whole. And even with all of the wisdom I receive in this channeled way, it can still take time for it to integrate fully. I mean, like, years. And so I continue on, enjoying what the relationship offers me while starting to feel really ungrounded.

By September, I am invited to attend a leadership retreat near the beach town of Puerto Viejo. I am told this is the best time of year to be on the Caribbean side. I invite Daniel to join me. Within a week of being there, my life changes drastically. Daniel, with whom I have been planning to relocate to the Pacific side next month, suddenly breaks up with me. A reason, a season, or a lifetime, right? Once again, I have lost the object of my love and the potential realization of my dream. And yet somehow, when he ends things, my immediate reaction is relief. Soon, though, the grief follows. I cry my tears, get angry, release what needs to be released, and accept the unacceptable.

As nature would have it, I have a few friends in town, and one of them lets me stay with her and her son while I sort things out. I find myself again debating a familiar question: Where will I live next? When I first arrived in the country in March, I spent about two weeks in this beach town. I didn't like it. It felt dirty, rundown, too exposed to the elements, too … jungly. Now, I'm here again and desperately want to leave, but, now flying solo again, I don't have anything else lined up. As much as I have come to accept my reality of being in Costa Rica (and have grown quite fond of living here), I don't see myself living in this part of it. I have something else in mind.

I can clearly see the type of house I want to live in—lots of windows, lots of light, overlooking the ocean, ideally with an infinity pool. I have already gotten a taste of this, traveling to various homes, visiting friends and clients, and living with Daniel for four months. I think I know exactly what I want, and I can't seem to find it here in Puerto Viejo. But then I learn of something on the other side of the country in Santa Teresa, a town I've heard great things about that seems like it'll be a better fit. A woman I recently met has found a two-bedroom place for us to rent. It is exactly what I've had in mind (without the infinity pool), so I say, "Yes!" I pay her for the first month and plan to meet her there in a week's time. Still a bit adamant that I am supposed to be living a certain way and in a certain type of house, by golly, I feel determined to make that happen! How quickly I have forgotten what I realized when I first arrived here.

Days after putting money down for the rental, locals start rioting in the streets in response to some new tax laws. Bridges and roadways are blocked as things are set on fire, slowing and at times completely halting traffic and general movement. Given the two-lane roads and limited modes of transportation within the country, this makes getting from one side to the other nearly impossible. But that doesn't keep me from trying. For days, I try to figure out a way to get to where I want to be.

Across the world, people's freedoms are still being "taken away," and here I am in one of the most "free" places, feeling like I'm being held hostage. Being in resistance to staying where I am and trying so desperately to leave only makes things worse. Freedom is not something outside of us to be given or taken away; it exists inherently within, and it is up to us to claim it or express it. My outer reality reflects back to me my inner reality. The world is not as it is, but as I am. This becomes even clearer as I recognize that, as free as I am, there are still ways I am imprisoning myself—I am hostage to my thoughts and beliefs. This is what keeps me "stuck."

When I first got to Costa Rica, I had a belief that the universe was just dragging me around and I was along for the ride. It's as though I subversively believed this is what it feels like to "follow" something. Somehow along the way, "following" felt outside of my control, and, therefore, when someone would ask why I moved to Costa Rica, I would say something like, "I got stuck here," or "The borders closed three days after I arrived." What's interesting about this is how I use language of entrapment to describe this experience of being perhaps the most free I've ever been in my entire life. Again, I haven't felt like a victim; I just haven't seen how not consciously choosing to live in Costa Rica doesn't mean I'm at the mercy of the universe. And how simply taking action based on what I feel guided to do and arriving in Costa Rica when I did, thanks to listening to the inner voice within, doesn't mean I'm being dragged around. So, again, I wonder if I am the actor or the writer. The pawn or the chessmaster? Or both?

Despite all the insights showing themselves to me, I still struggle. One gorgeous September day, I am sitting at my go-to beachside cafe, staring at the ocean that is still as glass. This time of year, this water is calm enough that swimmers can float carefreely, rocked only occasionally by a passing boat. Yet I find myself feeling so unhappy, even slightly depressed. I notice thoughts like, "What's the point? I'll never have what I want, no matter how hard I try." I feel I am being blocked from what I truly want (again). Yes, life is a series of repeated experiences. I've started to think we're on a merry-go-round until we return our physical body to the earth. I don't want to be in Puerto Viejo, and I am so frustrated that I'm not being more supported to leave. Staring out over the literal paradise of white sand and turquoise crystal clear water, I think, "If only I were in Santa Teresa, looking at *that* ocean, I'd be so much happier."

The thought stops me in my tracks. It is a not-so-subtle wake-up call. If I can't be happy here, where can I be happy? (Again, wherever I go, there I am.) Don't get me wrong, I'm not a proponent of always needing to be "happy." Happiness is a fleeting emotion; it is only one side of the mountain, one side of the wave. But I can clearly see my struggle to feel a certain way and how I look to my environment to provide me with that fleeting emotional response. It is important for me to reflect on when in my life I still look to my external world to create my happiness. We know this isn't where true joy is found. Now, the flip (and equally important) side to this is that just because I'm in a physical, external paradise doesn't mean I can't feel sad. People might say, "How can you be depressed in a place like this?!" to which I would say: "Because that is life. It's all of it. There are mosquitoes in paradise. And that's okay."

Can I instead remain in a state of non-attachment to both? Witnessing all of it? Enjoying the paradise and the depression, knowing that neither will last all too long, which means they will both return shortly? Just like the tide here comes in and goes out every six hours, reality transforms regularly. What good news! Nature is a true metaphor for the duality of life. We need to love and embrace our pain and sadness just as much as we love and embrace our pleasure and happiness. And it's not about loving it more, as in, "Oh, my gosh, I just *love* feeling depressed!" It's about holding both the pain and the pleasure more lightly. If I believe that paradise and pleasure and happiness and feeling good all the time are the only things worth living for, when I feel the opposite (which is inevitable), it will feel worth dying for.

After multiple attempts to leave Puerto Viejo to get to another side of paradise where I could finally be happy, I surrender. I arrive. I accept that this is where I am meant to be in this exact moment. I guess I'm staying. I have gotten clear on what I desire, "placed my order," and I am going to stop and let it come to me. How can I receive a package if I keep moving around all the time? Finally, I have "landed." I stay with my friend in her two-bedroom pink house in a small community called "Colores del Caribe," and what we initially think will be a five-week stay turns into more than five months living together before she and her son move into a new place of their own. I trust it is time to relax and stay put for a while, and, like always, I will be guided and supported on my path.

Even if it isn't exactly what I've had in mind, it is perfect for the moment. I have (fairly) reliable internet (some of the fastest in town!) and a roof over my head. I have amazing women living nearby with whom I connect deeply. I am surrounded by nature and even have a cat, Pedro, as a companion. I am learning what home truly is. And, to me, that doesn't require certain material comforts. I can feel comfortable wherever I go. It's how I've always been. I can walk into anyone's house, any hotel, any city or country and feel "at home." This often feels like a superpower, but it also has its drawbacks.

At this stage of my life, though, I desire to feel more settled and rooted. I start to worry that if I can be at home everywhere, does that mean home is actually nowhere? I then realize it also means I am always home. Home is where I am. More specifically, what I have learned is that home is where I am seen and known for who I truly am. Where there is nothing to prove.

PART 3

NON-CHOOSING

CHAPTER 13

GROWING ROOTS

Riding my bike down the jungle road on my way to meet my international, Caribbean-based family at the beach, the wind blowing through my hair, I notice tears of love and joy welling in my eyes. I am overwhelmed by how scary it is to feel this sort of love for others, this deep connection that I have been building here as if I am growing roots.

It has been more than a year since I arrived in Costa Rica. I have built a beautiful community of friends who feel like family. I have everything I need and want in this moment. I have a place to call home, fresh food to eat, people to love, people who love me, purposeful work to contribute to the world. I get to do what I love, work with amazing individuals, have amazing experiences. Each and every day. I am so blessed.

As I continue to take on new clients and publish more books (and see a larger vision for this company), I've hired additional team members to support me with Awaken Village Press. It feels amazing to have others working with me, also seeing my vision and helping me move towards it. I attend weekly dinner parties with friends, sit on my neighbor's porch having deep and meaningful conversations, go on waterfall hikes that leave me speechless, ride my bike each and every day to and from my favorite beachside spots, practice yoga and dance, receive tarot readings and energy work, watch fire spinners, learn Spanish, watch monkeys and sloths and toucans, eat delicious food, drink coconut water straight out of the coconut that I open with a machete, walk along the beach, listen to the sound of the ocean, float in the sea, and meet friends for drinks and dinner regularly. I am beyond grateful for all that I have, all that I am, and all that I receive.

For as much as I have wanted to feel I belong somewhere, the paradox is I have been afraid to grow attached to this community I am building here in Puerto Viejo. It feels unsafe, even crazy, to do so, knowing I will leave one day. This isn't my "forever" place; it is only temporary. So, why would I allow myself to feel so attached? Arriving at my beach destination to spend time with my friends, I am simultaneously feeling the fear and desire to know it is safe to be securely attached to this place and these beautiful souls while continuing to hold my dream and vision for the life I ultimately desire.

During a call with my mentor the following day, she reminds me how we are all capable of both creating and destroying. I have been doing some shadow work over the past year and am well aware of this ability I possess to destroy things. She invites me to look at my "destroyer" as a dragon. What I quickly realize is that dragons are also here to protect. There is an aspect of me who has been caged up, protected by this dragon. The dragon has been protecting this version of me who has deep desires, clear knowings and visions, and is securely attached to these co-creations. The dragon has shown up to protect this part of me by convincing me that it's best to remain non-attached and even at times to go for things I'm certain not to get. All of this is the peculiar way of protecting me from later feeling the pain of loss that I have become plenty familiar with. But guess what? That's right, you know this by now—there is loss no matter what. My dragon has ineffectively attempted to keep me from feeling loss by creating loss at the beginning ("I'll let it go before it lets me go"; "I'll keep moving so it can't find me"). Again, all from this place of believing it's unsafe to feel attached to something for fear that I will then one day lose it and hurt all the more.

As much as I appreciate the dragon's concern, it's obvious that it is no longer serving me. While I appreciate the collective's sentiment to "just let it go" or "release it" or "practice non-attachment" (a pillar I've lived my life by), I've taken it all too far. Perhaps I never quite understood it in the first place. "Amanda, you're attached to being non-attached," someone said to me many years ago. It resonated then and still plays out in my life today. Non-attachment, much like my need to know, has become more of a weapon than a tool. I'm learning that it's not about being attached or non-attached; it's about releasing myself from the fear of attachment. And for me to come into balance and fuller integration, I need to "hold on" just a bit more than I have before.

While lying in bed that night, stirred by a song I have been listening to, I start to feel into how my womb is a space of co-creation. The womb is a literal space, a container, for a baby (but also for dreams and visions) to take root and grow. Inside, it is attached by an umbilical cord. This secure connection is what feeds it, fuels it, strengthens it, ultimately nourishing and nurturing this developing being.

It is such a tricky thing to navigate. I mean, when a woman is pregnant, it's okay to be attached to that being coming through, to whether it's a boy or girl, and even to the name it's given. We don't tend to tell pregnant people, "Don't get too attached, now," even though we don't know what is going to happen or how it will all turn out. Of course, there is wisdom in not being overly attached to what the child will look like or if the child will become a doctor. But it's okay to be attached to the idea of giving birth to this exact child, this particular soul. It's okay to be securely attached to the idea of being this child's caregiver. But if I do that with a vision for, say, a particular partner, I might be described as "controlling" or "holding on too tightly."

There is a holding period, a time when the seed or dream stays safely protected to be nourished and nurtured by the womb. This doesn't take active effort or force. There is no "I'm making this baby grow!" or "I'm going to give this baby blue eyes!" There is simply a holding and an allowing. The holding is key. And this "holding" can often feel like "waiting." The seeds of new life, the keys to our dreams, are held in our womb space, and that is also where they grow and mature until they are ready to be released. If we let them go too early, we miscarry or abort the dream.

This concept gets me thinking. Much like with my trepidation toward getting too attached to my soul family here in Puerto Viejo, I find myself wavering between being attached to the vision of who my partner is (and knowing that I've already met him) and feeling like I have to completely let that go. It, too, feels unsafe—even crazy—to hold onto this vision.

If the vision for partnership is currently growing in my womb (and I must say it feels like I'm nearly at term), then can't I be attached (as is an umbilical cord) to that dream coming through and who that person might be just as I would with the child I'm about to birth? I am connected to the idea that, one day, this partnership with a soul I already know will be mature enough to manifest in the external world. I may not know exactly what this partnership will look like or what it will evolve into, but I can know it contains certain traits or qualities like I know a child will have hair on its head (at least for a few decades) and ten fingers and toes.

The same is true for my company and the vision I have held for it. You see, nearly three years ago, Clint, my friend and mentor from Sioux Falls, was the one to "impregnate" me with the idea of becoming a book doula and starting a company to help others write and publish their books. From the moment the idea was conceived, I held it in my womb. By the time I gave birth to Awaken Village Press, I already knew its name, what it could "look like," and its purpose in the world—a publishing company for transformational authors, awakening the planet one book at a time. These initial traits were chosen and known before it was "born." I needed to be securely attached to this vision in order for it to manifest. And now that it is in the world, it continues to grow and expand and evolve. At times, this isn't easy.

As I've said, the entrepreneurial path is not for the faint of heart. While I'm doing what I love and working with some amazing people, it's hard. I continue to find myself running out of money (and, this time, I have other people I am responsible for paying). I wake up with anxiety daily, which isn't a common experience for me. One thing I'm seeing more clearly is how I'm a creator, not a business operator. I haven't seemed to figure out how to run a successful company. As clear and exciting as my vision has been for what this company could one day be, the ups and downs are disheartening. I feel ready to throw in the towel and destroy what I've created.

I love the analogy of flowing down a river, letting it take me where it wants, but it's been pointed out to me that sometimes it's okay to steer as opposed to running into rocks or branches. I've often wondered why I don't resonate with the idea of using my arms to paddle my way through life. Alan Watts has helped me see where my hang-up might be. He compares the person who uses an oar (or their arms) to the sailor who erects a sail and uses the wind—the former exerts much effort; the latter uses magic. This makes so much sense—no wonder I haven't resonated with using an oar; that is synonymous with me efforting my way through life. But, as Watts points out, there is nothing wrong with cooperating with nature's flow and power. In all honesty, we can't *not* cooperate with nature—we are not separate from it. At this stage of my life, I see how this recurring theme of giving myself over to wherever the current takes me is beginning to feel more destructive than creative. It is time to raise my sails and hold onto the helm.

Over the next few weeks, with encouragement from team members and friends as well as some money finally flowing in, I stay the course, but I know something has to change. I need a partner. Much like how clear I am that I am not to go through life alone, I know I am not to raise this company alone. I am ready for a "father" to step in and help at this point in its development. It no longer needs me and me alone for its sustenance. It's a toddler now, and this is the weaning phase. Now, I still have a role to play as its mother, and it is safe to have a healthy attachment to it as something that came through me and that I desire to grow into something spectacular. So, I start to get clear on what I want and who I am calling in to support me.

There is tremendous power in the co-creation, the partnership between the feminine and masculine. Certainly, this can occur within one body; but it can also be tremendously powerful when it is embodied in another (like when a man and woman come together). I'm clear that what I want is to partner with the masculine embodied in the form of a man to bring my dreams into reality. I believe that in doing so, this also offers the masculine greater fulfillment and satisfaction. The masculine needs the feminine embodied as a woman as much as the woman needs the masculine embodied as a man to draw forth from him what he truly wants and then give him the opportunity to bring it into reality.

Soon after knowing what I know to be true, one day in the fall of 2021, I receive a message from Clint. We hop on a call to catch up on life and, by the end of it, I realize he is the one I want to step forward and play the role. As someone who gets me and has been in the entrepreneurial world for decades, it makes perfect sense (and he is the inspirational "father" after all). I ask if he is willing to step into this role as partner with me and, after some consideration, he says yes. Shortly thereafter, my brother (another significant masculine in my life) supports me once again to help grow the business by serving as a financial investor. With this immediate security, I am able to hold on a bit more to this creation.

I must "slay the dragon" and release this innocent being, this part of me who is here to support me in living a fully integrated life, who no longer needs to be protected because what she has to offer me is great. I am creating space for this aspect of myself, this person in me who can be securely attached to an idea, place, or person (and, most importantly, my vision) to come out and play—not living from a place of fear. This part of me is the creator of what I want. She envisions it and holds onto it—without having control over how it comes to fruition.

And 2021 certainly has been a year of "fruition." While not everything in my journal entries has come to be exactly as I've written about, many things have manifested. Now, this has certainly not been without periods of darkness. Still, despite those periods, I have experienced so much joy and gratitude and expansion and manifestation—just as duality would have it.

Releasing my attachment to non-attachment, I am experiencing greater freedom. By having committed to holding onto my desires (because doing so is as safe to do as anything else), I am also experiencing greater freedom. It is safe to be attached to my dream that Awaken Village Press will grow and mature into a successful, impactful company. And just like having a child, we cannot guarantee these things. It is painful when things don't evolve the way we hope, yet the anticipation of pain shouldn't keep us from holding the vision and remaining connected to it. Now, if only I could feel this safe being attached to my beloved and bring into reality my home and my child.

As much as I love the life I have built for myself here and have come to peace with being securely attached to it, I feel ready to leave the safety and security of this place I have surrendered and rooted into for over the past eighteen months. Come next July, the property owner will no longer be offering long-term rentals, and the house I've been living in won't be available. Another reminder that nothing lasts forever. As soon as I can travel freely and without external restrictions, I will steer myself to the next stop along the river and find a new home. I feel it is coming soon.

By the end of the year, I make plans to travel in May back to Vicenza, the home I had chosen two summers ago. The timing seems to once again be divinely guided. My original plan to return to Italy in April 2020 had coincided with my parent's fiftieth-anniversary cruise through Europe, which, due to global restrictions, had also been postponed to May 2022, right before I would need to vacate my home. The plan is to meet my family in Venice and show them around the place I claimed as home. I've spent nearly two years in this paradise, returning to my true nature, experiencing the fullness and balance life has to offer. And now, realizing that paradise is not a physical location but an inner state of being, I look forward to bringing it with me wherever I may go and sharing its transformative effects with others.

As I'm thinking about my upcoming return to Italy, I receive a text from Grace. It's a stealth photo she had taken of a chance encounter with my Italian man. Seeing the photo of him brings up a lot—is this a sign from the universe? Am I supposed to keep the faith after all? I hadn't thought of him much since I was in Italy and he was constantly on my mind. I don't know what to do with it—I don't want to make it mean more than it does.

During my time in Costa Rica, I've let myself be open to meeting and expressing my love with other men even though I haven't actively been looking for them. I haven't kept my heart closed, and I don't want to start now. Each one seems to embody what I want, even if none of them are the man I had met and chosen in Sioux Falls.

Given the number of men I've connected with, I often wonder whether a soul (or its essence) can appear in many different bodies. I wonder if perhaps the energy of the masculine (or of the soul) that I am meant to be with has been showing up in various forms for me. It makes sense in some ways, given I feel I am here to love the masculine in all its expressions. If that is the case, can my beloved's energy be manifesting in these different men for me so that my heart can stay connected to what it desires?

Still, what if my staying open to others is what is keeping Michael from returning to me? Equally, what if I close my heart to others and he never returns? It's not easy for me sometimes, but I find myself leaning into a saying that helps me relax: "What is meant for me will not pass me by."

So, perhaps I can relax and trust a bit more. Even if I don't always see it at first, I seem to be put where I'm meant to be. I mean, look where I've ended up living. After all my deliberating and decision-making resulted in choosing Italy as my new home base, I ended up in Costa Rica for more than two years—exactly where I needed to be at this time in my life. Sometimes what we want ends up coming in a different form or at a different time.

CHAPTER 14

HOLDING THE VISION

Overlooking the white sand and turquoise water (a bit choppier now that it is January), I am once again at my favorite beachside cafe, dancing, laughing, drinking, and having lovely conversations. I'm celebrating a friend's birthday when a tall, handsome man walks in. I take note of him on the spot. He has an energy about him. We end up chatting as best we can, given he is primarily a German speaker and I am not at all. Talking with him, I'm disarmed. All of a sudden, I can't prove how smart or intellectual I am with words since we share so few in common. I start to see my attachment to talking as a way of connecting with another. And this man, in particular, is one of few words (at least with English speakers). But it doesn't matter. I immediately sense a deep connection with him, a feeling that's so familiar by now yet still special each time. The words aren't important. I realize that verbal communication, as much as I love it and rely on it heavily at times, isn't everything. There is something else, something deeper, that can be experienced when we let words go. When we sit in silence, we feel the other person.

Andre has no wife and no children. He makes good money and works for himself. He travels and sails around the world. I admire how he has the ability to both go with the flow and cooperate with nature. His life is, by many standards, the epitome of freedom. He's adventurous and financially secure. He's positive and funny. He doesn't take himself or life too seriously. He is playful and enjoys nice things. He accepts life as it is. His favorite phrase is: "It is what it is." In so many ways, he is an embodiment of what I am and desire.

After meeting me, he extends his time in Puerto Viejo a few extra days before continuing his travels around Costa Rica. He promises he'll come back to see me before returning to Germany, maybe for my 40th birthday party in just under two months. Like the story of the Chinese farmer, he often says, "Maybe," a smirk spreading across his face. When he leaves to continue his adventures, I send him off with a kiss, a smile, and a "see you soon." In contrast to the last time I kissed a man goodbye before he flew back home, this time, I am confident he will be coming back. It brings my tender, open heart relief to lean into this belief. But as his trip continues, I learn that his plans are shifting. He needs to get back sooner than he thought and is unsure if he can make it to my birthday. I accept this fact, trusting that if I am meant to see him again, I will. I feel I have (once again) attracted a version of exactly what I want in this tall German, and (once again) would need to let go of control and simply trust.

But then it starts. Little by little, day after day, the intensity of the fear and uncertainty grows stronger and stronger. He keeps me updated on his whereabouts, so in some ways, it is different this time. He stays connected by sending photos. And if a picture is worth a thousand words, I suppose he is very communicative indeed. After about a week of this, I start to feel the deep wound of mine begin to open and feel exposed. I start getting nervous that he isn't going to return. I begin to doubt everything he has said and everything I have felt. I start to get anxious and worried. Soon, it turns into an emotional, hot ball of anxiety in my solar plexus, and tears start to flow and release. I start sending more messages (not as many as I might have in the past, but still more than I had been with him). I start talking to friends about it and seeking advice. I start meditating and sending him love. The pain doesn't subside. It's not the "not having him" or "him not being here" that's the most fear-inducing piece—I mean, he left, and I'm super excited for him to be exploring and surfing and traveling and doing his thing. It's not that I need him here by my side. It's the loving him and not knowing what will happen. It's my fear of love, keeping me stuck in this cycle—my fear that my love won't be returned or will be for naught.

Reminiscent of my first time in Costa Rica, most mornings I sit on my front porch, sipping my coffee, looking at the palm trees, and listening to mind-expanding lectures as Pedro purrs beside me. In this particular one, Alan Watts talks about how it's when we're "sticky"— when we aren't moving smoothly, like a bike chain that is caught—that something forms into an attachment. Enjoying a meal is natural. Wanting to sleep is natural. Desiring love and sex is natural. Desiring connection and comfort is natural. Loving another is natural. Not knowing what will happen (and even being uncomfortable with that) is natural. It is my fear of uncertainty and need to know that catches me. I'm afraid to love another fully, no matter what that means, because I'm afraid of what it could mean.

The experience of attachment comes with a feeling of fear. There are a couple ways this can show up. One: we hold on for dear life out of fear that if we don't, we'll lose the very thing we love—a person, a house, a pet, a child, our own lives. Two: we push things away (some-times unconsciously) because we fear that we will eventually lose them, so it's better to never have them in the first place. The painful reality is that both perspectives are correct—we will lose the very thing we love … eventually. But we get to choose if we love it fully now in this very moment because, in this very moment, it exists or if we try to prevent the loss of it. When we love something truly, we release our grip on it, we flow with it and the outcome, we don't force it. Much like using a sail, we are working with nature, not pushing or pulling the sail ourselves but allowing the wind to do the work. If we're holding on too tight, we don't allow the act of love to enter. Equally, if we are pushing something away out of fear, we block true love from flowing.

I identify as having an anxious attachment style, and I've tried to free myself of this pattern for years, yet it doesn't seem to go far. One thing I've learned is if there is something holding us back or that we desire to free ourselves from—a belief, a pattern, a person, an object—it is only by loving it that we can release ourselves from it (or it from us). Because release isn't so much an action as it is an outcome. As a wise friend of mine says, "Love it free." These two things seem to go hand-in-hand: love and freedom. Just as Ayahuasca showed me, we can't force release—it's two equally opposing energies that will become entangled and, therefore, keep something more stuck. The harder you pull your finger out of a Chinese finger trap, the tighter it gets. The same thing happens with our deeply ingrained beliefs and patterns. We can't force ourselves to stop believing or doing something. So long as we believe we are unsafe without our beliefs, we can't release ourselves from them. So long as I think I'm unsafe being attached, I can't release myself from the pattern of anxious attachment. Once I love and accept that I am attached to someone (and realize I'm okay), the part of me who feels insecure or thinks it is unsafe to love someone no longer needs to protect me. Nearly six years later, I think the wisdom of the vine is taking root in my being.

When I am not insecurely attached to something (as I am with most men), I am free to love it fully. What if I begin to more deeply understand and experience that by loving something more (which doesn't always feel comfortable), I am not anxiously attached to it but rather freeing myself and it, trusting that it will come and go as it pleases? I am free to love someone or something no matter what happens to it (or me). If I love someone from a secure place, I can show up fully as my loving self no matter the circumstances. I can say the things that may feel hard or vulnerable to say. I can open my heart completely. I can share my truth. I can express my boundaries. I can let them go.

I'm beginning to better understand what true non-attachment is, which is not my understanding that had been based in fear. If I live my life from a non-attached place, I can live each and every moment as it is. I can breathe in all that life has to offer me, not fearing that my life might end (because I know it eventually will, and I'm not attached to it). I can "live as if there's no tomorrow" because I'm not attached to whether I see tomorrow or not. Living from a place of non-attachment actually allows me to experience the depths of what secure attachment provides, to love more deeply, truly, and fully than ever before. If I look at my life and even my recent experiences with Andre and the men who came before him from this perspective, loving for love's sake is a beautiful thing. I am here to love. And I am so loved. Love is always returned, one way or another, because I am loving the divine and, therefore, loving myself. Love is never for naught. Love is a powerful gift.

Non-attachment does not mean not experiencing life. The exact opposite is true. We can experience all that life has to offer us like never before. As I enjoy my last few weeks of being in my thirties, I feel the secret to non-attachment isn't to not have any desires or wants—it's continuously flowing with whatever arises, whether it's the feeling of desire, the feeling of pain or loss, the feeling of joy, the feeling of anger, and then, beyond the feelings, the actions as well. To reach out, to respond, to pull back, to lean in, to move forward, to move back, to cry, to scream, to laugh, to moan, to get excited, to be disappointed, to say "I love you," to say "I'm sorry," to create, to destroy, to rebuild.

So what if this is my opportunity to love a man I just met (and have spent less than a week with) more deeply, more truly, more fully, even though I am uncertain about what will happen next? What if, instead of resisting my feelings and my love, I'm being asked to lean into them even more? This might appear on some level that I'm becoming more attached, and in some ways, I am—I am becoming more secure in my attachment. Equally, it is a new practice for me, so I am still finding my way. I want to be free to speak my heart's desires and not be attached to the outcome, even if I'm allowing myself to be attached to what I want (the former is a future moment that I can't control, the latter is the now moment and all there is).

It has been a few weeks since the tall German left. I decide I'm going to speak into my desire to see him one more time before he flies back home. I feel excited and giddy to send the message, but before hitting the button that would send it off into the technical abyss, I pause. I hesitate. I doubt myself. I go into all the reasons I shouldn't send it: I'm forcing things. I'm coming on too strong. I'm not allowing him to "chase" me or come to me. I'm too much in my masculine right now. I'm coming off too eager and available. And on and on and on. Then, I quiet these fears and hit send. This is what I want to free myself from—the incessant noise and doubt and fear and insecurity. It's a goddamn text message! And yet, it can feel like it's the biggest deal in the world sometimes.

I am intentionally releasing myself from one of my shackles as I send the message. I let go and let it be. I desire to be a woman who is free to express herself and doesn't require others to respond in a certain way (or at all). A day goes by and he doesn't respond to my message. And I'm okay with that. I love myself and my courage and freedom of expression and enthusiasm for this man to be in my life. I celebrate that I'm continuously becoming more and more relaxed in my interactions with men. I'm trusting more, letting go more—not necessarily of what I want or need but of how it needs to go.

I acknowledge that whoever will partner with me will understand that sometimes I get excited, sometimes I come on strong because I express my desires, taking action rather than just sitting and waiting. And he will still love me. In addition, he'll see it as an opportunity to step in and take charge more often. He'll see those moments as an offering or opportunity to take more action so that I can go back into my receptive, relaxed energy.

Thirty-six hours after sending that message, as I'm about to get ready for bed, my front door opens. In walks a tall, handsome German with a smirk on his face. I literally gasp out loud. I had no idea he was coming back as I hadn't heard from him. Apparently, he drove over four hours one way to see me for a few hours before driving back to catch his flight to Germany. I ask him why he came back, and he says, "Because I promised I would return." Tears fill my eyes. This feels like a significant message being delivered to me from the universe through a masculine body.

For much of my life, I haven't trusted the masculine. I've had so many stories that the masculine lets me down and doesn't follow through on his word. And yet, here's a man who I've only spent a few nights with who is willing to drive more than ten hours round trip to see me. Why? Because he said he would. Now, that's a man of his word. After dancing and playing cards and making love, he gets back in his car and drives off. I have no idea if I'll ever see him again.

Andre has offered me the gift of relaxing more deeply into my receptivity, trusting my heart's desires, and experiencing the inspired action that comes from that place. The feminine speaks her desires out loud. She proclaims them, she makes them known, she inspires the masculine to make them manifest. And this man rose to the challenge—he has answered the call to step into greater action, make the effort, and uphold his promise to me that he would see me again. He has crossed the moat for me. He was free to take charge and come back to me, and he followed his heart's desires, possibly spurred and inspired by me expressing mine. When I inhibit myself or keep myself from expressing my own heart's desires, I keep the masculine from being free to make those dreams a reality. When I free myself, I free him to play his essential role.

It seems I am finally allowing myself to feel worthy and deserving of experiencing more of who I am and what I want—men who are reliable, financially stable, and willing to share that with me and others. I'm getting more confident and assured about what I desire, which means having greater certainty about what I want. I am beginning to experience a life I had envisioned for myself in some very tangible ways. My external reality is once again reflecting my inner reality. What I value and believe (and possess within) are being reflected back to me in the outer world. I am beginning to realize once and for all I don't need to *do* anything more to have it in my life—I just have to *be* it.

I've been learning that what we value, we will attract in our lives. And values can change, so it's natural for us to change our minds at times about even serious decisions. The following week, with forty just around the corner, I sit down and write out what I value most at this stage of my life. I've started to prioritize my value for security, which comes in many forms. First and foremost, internally, in feeling free to express myself and trusting it is safe to do so. But also externally, represented by resources, the masculine energy, and feeling provided for. This is another value I have started to prioritize—being in my feminine receptivity.

Within hours of reflecting on what I value and desire most, I glance at my phone to see I've received an email. "Can we please talk?" reads the subject line. It's from the man in Vicenza. It's been nearly two and a half years since we last had contact. Immediately, tears fill my eyes, and I cover my mouth as I begin to chuckle in disbelief. A handful of times, I have touched what I call "truth." It comes in the form of pure physical paradox, equal parts laughing and crying simultaneously. It's quite a bizarre experience, but it is familiar by now. It has happened during breathwork and plant medicine sessions or as I stare up at the Costa Rican night sky when I have been taken over by the full both/and experience of life. *Ananda.* Bliss. Now, I feel it again in my body. The visceral and emotional experience integrates these moments of truth more in my being.

I open the email. He apologizes for his previous behavior, for pushing me away in August 2019 and blocking me. "Amanda, it would mean the world to me if you would give me an opportunity to talk with you. You've never left my heart or mind, even after my last message to you when you courageously came to Italy with your entire heart. You haven't been forgotten. Love, Michael." The universe seems to have a few things it wants me to know at this particular time in my life—and once again, they are being delivered to me in the form of the masculine. The energy I feel is intense. I'm completely shocked and simultaneously not at all. I'm terrified and equally thrilled.

I remember what a mentor of mine said: "Words aren't the truth; they simply point to the truth." The truth is simple. But, when we aren't in person to feel each other or touch each other, words are what we've got. I think about my wordless communication with Andre, and the word-exclusive message I'm now getting from Michael. They both mean so much in their own ways.

He gives me his number and requests I contact him. We spend three hours catching up and reconnecting over video. He still isn't available.

Their marriage hasn't officially ended, but they haven't shared a bed for more than a year and plan to separate physically once he retires before the end of the year. I have "placed an order," and the universe has not lost or forgotten my delivery. I've simply needed to wait for the time when it would arrive. Finally, here he is.

Our reunion brings up a lot of things I feel I had already worked through. Am I falling into an old pattern, or am I receiving everything I ever wanted? There's something about this man that activates a desire deep within me to claim him. I experience a very deep knowing (different from others with whom I have felt something similar, even the handsome German, whom I haven't heard from since he left, and the unavailable Costa Rican who shared a past life with me). But I'm not sure what this knowing means. What if I commit to my truth that it is him, share that, and get rejected … again? It's that "again" that feels the most terrifying, vulnerable, and foolish.

Listening to Alan Watts (a teacher Michael and I share in common) discuss Zen Buddhism during my morning porch routine, he talks about "not being phased" as another way of explaining "not being attached." He refers to a Japanese Okiagari doll, which is a symbol of perseverance and resilience. This feels like my life. I get pushed down, rejected, broken-hearted, and I choose to rise again. It reminds me of what I channeled during my inner dialogue the last time I had contact with Michael: *I'm tired of proving my resiliency. I know I'm resilient. I've fallen and gotten back up so many fucking times by this point. When can I finally stay upright?!*

I feel how terrified I still am of trusting myself and opening my heart in this way again. It's been broken so many times. But what if everything I've ever wanted is on the other side of this fear? This belief that it isn't for me? Instead of letting my fear of fully loving get the better of me, I use what I have recently learned about myself and open my heart even more. I write him a brief love note expressing this sentiment: "Like a legless Japanese doll, I am not fazed by your current circumstances. If I'm knocked over seven times, I'll rise eight. This seems to be a superpower of mine and one I'm willing to employ as often as necessary. I will keep being kind. It is my nature. I will keep dreaming. It is my nature. I will keep expressing my love and desires. It is my nature. I will keep being patient. It is (becoming) my nature. We do not know the 'how' or 'when' of all this, and I am okay with that. All I know is there is something that brought us together and brought you back to me. And this same 'something' is what is guiding me still. Focus on what you need to focus on. Decide what you need to decide. Take care of what you need to take care of. Take the lead, and I will follow." Even though I am nervous to commit my heart to him, I accept the reality of the situation and wait it out. Yet the question still lingers: How long will I need to wait?

Less than a week later, I'm at a hotel in San José, waiting for my parents to arrive for my birthday festivities. As I wait, I listen to some of the messages I recorded for myself about Michael nearly three years prior. In one of these audio journals, I promise to wait for him. I start sobbing in the hotel room. I imagine this feeling in my heart is fear or heartbreak, but what if it's love? Is there anything that isn't? Even heartbreak is the awareness of just how much love I feel for someone. A broken heart and a heart breaking open with love produce a very similar sensation.

At first, listening to what I said all those years ago, I feel like I had lied, like I had said one thing and then done another. I didn't wait for him. I lived my life—fully. I've fallen in love many times with others since. Hell, I even thought I met the man of my dreams just four weeks earlier. I said I would wait and then did anything but! And then I consider what I realized about "waiting" when I first arrived in Costa Rica: What if this *is* what waiting looks like? I *have* waited because here I am, my heart still open.

What it means to "claim him" and "wait for him," while still scary, have taken on new meanings. What if it has never been "up to me" because there has always been a larger plan and timeline that I am not privy to? But I still don't know what to make of all this or if I am being crazy, doing it all over again.

As if on cue, I receive a message from Michael sharing a link to a video from our favorite philosopher. His words speak directly to my soul.

"What is really sensible is to let go, to give oneself up, and that's quite mad. So we come to the strange conclusion that in madness lies sanity."

Being thousands of miles apart from where he is feels challenging at times. Part of my vision was that I would be with my beloved for my big day. I have been holding the vision for quite some time about my 40th birthday. I've gotten clear on how I want to celebrate this milestone event, and nearly everything's coming together for me to experience what I want. Numerous friends and family celebrating in a bright, open, white, beach-side house with a pool, beautiful decor, a fantastic DJ, and delicious food (provided by another very dear man in my life). The party is amazing, with many people who have come from far and wide. I feel so loved and celebrated and supported. Still, something is missing.

For as close as I've gotten to manifesting my beloved's presence, it doesn't come to fruition. I wish he had been able to come and complete the vision I've been holding, but I understand that it felt impossible for him to make a trip like that on such short notice (not to mention how he would have explained it). As my arrival date in Italy gets nearer, we continue to exchange numerous messages, making plans and sharing how we want our reunion to feel the day after I land. I long to connect with him physically, not just with words.

One morning, sitting on my porch, big, fat, warm tears roll down my cheeks as I wonder what connection truly is. What does it mean to connect or experience connection? I've learned while journeying with DMT how important and essential physical connection is—it's one of the reasons we are in these physical bodies. And it's okay to long for that, to desire that, to have that. It's part of living fully, experiencing it all. But I can't have that right now with Michael. Am I trying to fill that void by communicating more? I do know we are never *not* connected since everything is interconnected. I've experienced connecting with souls and energy even when I'm not physically present with someone. I've experienced telepathy and what it feels like to be connected to all that is. So is it my lack of belief in this knowing that drives my need for evidence of it?

This inner dialogue reminds me that I'm still trying to "figure out" why being human is uncomfortable and what I can do to change it. I tell myself that if I just connect with or talk to or see him, I'll feel more comfortable, as opposed to simply accepting the discomfort. That's it. It doesn't mean I'm not connected to him and all that is. Sometimes connection is comfortable, even pleasurable, and sometimes it's uncomfortable, even painful.

You see, I continue to believe matters of the heart can be understood. But they can't. I have thought that if I am clear about something, specifically what I want, I have to be coherent or logical. That would ensure I understand what things mean and why they work the way they do, as well as prove that I'm worthy of receiving what I desire. What I am beginning to realize is that it's simpler than that. I don't have to understand something in order to receive it or have it (and just because I do doesn't mean I will). All I need to do is know what I know, hold that vision without confusion or doubt (the actual definition of "clear"), and let go of the outcome. And while I am still not in control of what he chooses or by when, I can control my willingness to relax and wait rather than rush the outcome I desire. I am willing to give myself up and let him take the lead, trusting whatever is meant to be will be.

This is what I'm being asked to do: surrender to all that life has to offer me, to feel and live it all, to take the next step and then the next without having any clear understanding of why it's unfolding this way or what's to come next. I don't want to be the one in control anymore. I'm being asked to love fully and continue to be with the discomfort and uncertainty of life. That's it. There's nothing to fix or force or better understand. Understanding or rationalizing it won't make it less uncomfortable. I can free myself from this so as to free myself to be more human, to feel and experience all things, including discomfort and pain.

As I start this new decade of my life, it's time to once again spread my wings and fly, trusting that the wind will carry me. The time has come to say goodbye to Costa Rica (for now) and return to Italy. It also means I get to have another "Ciao for Now" party. Four of my closest girlfriends and I gather for an Italian dinner to share stories, honor the deep relationships we have formed, and salute the next leg of my journey. For how scared I seem to be of building connection with people, I sure do it often and easily. Ah, the paradox of life.

Traveling to Italy this time does not require external signs to guide me or confirm my decision. I simply make the choice and act, and the universe conspires to meet me. The same Airbnb I lived in when I was last in Vicenza happens to be available for the exact amount of time I need it, including the downstairs unit, where I will host my family for a week. Travel mandates are lifted right in time for my trip. I'm not "choosing" Italy, and I'm not "choosing" to leave. I'm responding to stimuli—my Costa Rica house is no longer available, my parents are traveling to Europe this month, and Grace is getting married in Tuscany this September. I'm simply letting life unfold and guide me as I accept or resist what is being presented to me. I still don't know what's going to happen, but I know it will unfold and be revealed exactly as it's meant to each step of the way.

CHAPTER 15

RETURNING HOME

Flying thousands of feet in the air, I ask myself: Are you okay following your desires, not knowing how things will turn out? My answer: yes. It's okay to have desires and remain securely attached to them even though I never know what the outcome will be. My heart is leading me, and I continue to follow that. The rest will be what it is. Don't get me wrong; that is really damn hard. And sometimes painful. Just because I'm letting love lead doesn't mean I don't feel some of the deepest pain or heartache (and this might be exactly *why* I can endure it). I can handle everything because I am willing to feel everything. What I can't handle is not following my desires any longer.

May is a beautiful time to be returning to Vicenza. There are parallels and differences to when I flew to Italy nearly three years prior. Back then, I hadn't yet started to see things as part of a happening. I hadn't yet questioned the meaning I was ascribing to things as they unfolded in my life (or let there be no meaning). I hadn't yet learned how to let things be. This time, I have a deeper knowing. I have been able to zoom out and see how everything is working out according to some larger plan, one that I had a glimpse of years earlier but less control over than I thought. And still, I am putting myself back in the same position I put myself in then, when my heart got broken and I wondered if I could truly trust myself. This time, I'm not afraid of that. I've already felt that pain and fully faced that fear. Now, I won't blame myself for choosing my heart, even if things don't go the way I want. The outcome could be different this time, or it could be exactly the same.

While I'm not traveling to Italy for Michael, my soul is delighted by the possibility of seeing him again. That the things I had desired on my first trip there may finally come to fruition. I mean, I eventually did receive a yoni egg (albeit a different one, in Costa Rica), and my friend Grace has been storing my podcast mic (which finally arrived in Vicenza). And just like I wasn't in control of when or how I received these things, the same continues to apply to the man.

I think back to my old patterns of control. Ayahuasca showed me that there's nothing bad or wrong with controlling my experience. I used to see it as being synonymous with taking radical responsibility for my life. And it served me well for quite some time. I learned how to modify my breath or thoughts or reactions in order to experience something different, to experience myself as the observer. What I am beginning to understand all these years later is that this still assumes there is a part of me that is separate and able (or needing) to control these things. There is no separate part of me that needs to be in control, and believing this is true is what keeps me stuck. Instead, I can trust that an action or behavior or thought or expression is part of something larger than me. I am all of it—my thoughts and feelings and sensations and emotions, an expression of the universe experiencing itself. In this way, there is nothing to "control." That, much like it's not about controlling other people's thoughts, behaviors, and actions, the same can apply to my own. I can let them all be. I'm a part of the dance. I'm one with nature, not needing to create a particular type of nature.

But then, I wonder, who am I if I no longer control things? Believing I can control an outcome by attempting to control myself or others has been part of my identity for a long time. So what would happen if I stopped trying to control things? Well, that's a lot of time that I now don't have to worry and fret and expend energy on something in order to feel a certain way. What if I choose to feel safe and secure within, no matter what happens around me? Isn't that what my inner masculine is here for? To remind me that I am always safe and secure no matter what? What if, instead of controlling things, I let go and trusted that what needs to get done will get done?

Something about flying above the earth offers me a wider perspective. Reflecting on the past few months, I see where I am still challenged by this. Despite all that I am learning and unlearning, I still feel uncertain about how much trust I can place in others (or in my intuition). In my company, I have been facing deeper beliefs around delegating responsibility, continuously worrying whether my colleagues are taking care of their tasks. In romantic relationships, I fret over whether or not the man I'm interested in will contact me, still thinking it's all up to me. This is something I've had to look square in the face, specifically since meeting Michael. Since he appeared in my life on a street in Sioux Falls, I've been shown time and time again how I'm truly not in control in the way I think I am and can't force things the way I sometimes want. I was not in control when he sat next to me at the restaurant or found a way to contact me. I couldn't convince him to not block me. I couldn't (nor did I try to) force him to contact me again out of the blue a few months prior. And here I am again, unable to control what decision he makes or in what timing he makes it, trusting that the universe is listening and my dreams are being made manifest.

Why do I continue to worry if I'll ever have a life-long partner or if my company will be a seven-figure company? Why do I feel the need to be in a state of fear and anxiety? Why do I choose to feel insecure about what others will or will not do? So often we talk about the importance of feeling secure in ourselves, so why can we not extend that security to our entire lives?

You see, becoming free isn't just about *me* becoming free; it's also about me freeing others and freeing myself from others. When I'm controlling something, I'm not free and neither is the thing or person I am controlling. Control imprisons, entrapping all those who are involved. Becoming free is not just breaking free from the illusion or perception that others are controlling me; it is breaking free from the control I exert in the world around me.

It's been over two years since I've been on a plane, and, just as I declared I would months prior, I am traveling freely, without masks or mandates. Merely weeks before, Italy and other countries began lifting the travel restrictions that could have kept me from entering the country and postponed, yet again, my parents' anniversary trip. It's as if I am creating my own reality, and seeing what happens when I don't live by doubt delights me. But creating my own reality doesn't mean I'm in control in the way I once thought. So how do I create the reality I want without exerting control? Is that even up to me? Thanks to a dear friend and astrologer of mine, I've received some insight on this, but the question still stumps me. You see, Pisces rules my fifth house, which is how I create in the world. Pisces is all about the bigger picture and how everything is connected. It sees the simultaneous vastness and unity. This means I create by connecting to spiritual truths and the divine. I create through faith. So, yes, I do create my own reality, but it will look and feel very different from someone who, say, has Aries ruling their fifth house. I'm not trying to teach astrology here but rather point out that there are many different ways we each approach creating our reality. For me, it is not "in my control"; you could say it is "out of my hands," as that is what Pisces represents.

Astrology is one tool I have used to understand this thing called life. It often helps me to relax and surrender. There are many tools we can use along the way to help us remember we aren't ultimately in control in the way we think we are. We can use prayer, meditation, yoga, plant medicine, breathwork, astrology, vision boarding, nearly any religious activity. These have all played (and at times still do) important roles in waking me up and loosening my grip, remembering that I am a part of something so much larger. Yet, if we aren't careful, the very tool we pick up to help us learn to let go can become the very thing that keeps us stuck. Remember, a hammer can both help and harm. So, as much as I value what astrology teaches me, I also need to be careful not to let it become one more thing I use to feel in control.

Back when I asked my sun in Pisces to speak to me (yes, I do things like this sometimes), this is what it said: "The world is constantly changing, and so am I. Nothing is constant. The ability to adapt and flow is essential and so beautiful. The greatest gifts come from being willing to go with the flow and see what the universe has in store for you. You can trust your intuition as you see how all is connected, part of Source. You (and everything else) are part of all that is. In this way, everything is perfect and unfolding as it is meant to. Just because you flow and adapt easily, know that you are reliable just like change is reliable—meaning we can trust it will happen."

Now, try creating from a perspective like this! What a gift and challenge it can be, having faith and connection to something much larger than me deeply woven into how I create. Essentially, I was born to rely on others to bring into form that which I desire to create; all I have to do is sit back, wait, and pray to God they receive the memo. No biggie, right?! But, in all seriousness, there can be a feeling of restlessness in having faith and allowing the ripple effect to unfold, in holding the vision and allowing others to "do the work," which I can't control. And this is in every aspect of my life—my partnership, my business, my creative projects, my vision for having a family.

The story I have told myself and continued to recreate up until recently is that if I'm not the one doing something, it won't get done (or it will get done poorly). I'm ready to release this yet am unsure what that looks like. Does it mean I let things fall apart and be shitty? Does it mean I trust it will get done eventually? After years of being the one running the show and doing all the work, it feels foreign (and equally refreshing) not to be the one in charge anymore. What the past few years (and, more recently, months) have taught me is that it is safe to rest and slow down. When I do, things do not crumble; they become more alive. I can delegate power and control to others (in this way, I'm actually delegating power and control to my self, as we are all connected and all one). There is a much larger divine plan at play right now—it is not up to me to keep the world spinning. I give thanks to the part of me who felt that for so long. I now invite her to rest, relax, trust, and surrender even more.

Having drifted off to sleep, exhausted by my overactive thoughts, I wake up as the flight crew prepares us for landing. Arriving back in

Vicenza, I feel like I'm coming home. I roll my suitcase from the train station through the park toward the narrow cobblestoned streets that I recognize so well. I am jet-lagged and excited for what life has in store for me—this time around. While my surroundings look and feel the same, so many things have shifted and changed internally.

Within twenty-four hours of being back, I have another huge growth opportunity (shocking, I know!). It's the 16th of May. Another full moon, and this time, it's also a lunar eclipse in Scorpio. There's a lot that can be said about this (by a trained astrologer), but all you need to know is it's a potent time. I have plans to meet with the man I am so excited to reunite with. He says he'll be at my apartment at 6:00 a.m. He's an early bird, and I'm jet-lagged, so I go with the plan.

It's the first time I'll be seeing him since August 3, 2019, and I do all the things. I make a playlist. I shave. I light candles. I prepare myself and the space. At 6:10, he hasn't come. By 6:15, I know deep in my body and bones that he won't. I don't want to know that. I want to have faith. If I hold the faith, maybe he'll still come. If I know he isn't coming, then he won't. See how that works? Even after everything, I still believe I can control the outcome.

Neil Donald Walsh says, "Freedom is not getting what you want but wanting what you get." This is rooted in acceptance of what is. See, I have had all these stories and beliefs and thoughts around "getting what I want" and wanting things in the first place. I have fluctuated between not wanting anything (because I don't get it) to wanting something deeply and then being sad when I don't get it. What the fuck?

There's a natural progression from, and maybe a misunderstanding about, what it means to desire things and "not have things." There seems to be a strong school of thought (which isn't wrong) that it's important not to focus on what you don't have and also to remember we have everything we need within. Here's my current position on this: First of all, it's important to arrive at a point where we feel and believe that we already have everything we want or need. Why? Because this shifts us from believing something outside of us will make us happy or content or "okay." I believe this is the main reason we are taught to "find everything within." Arriving at a point on our journey where we stop looking to other people, things, or experiences to bring us happiness or fulfillment or satisfaction is critical. This supports us in remembering that we are always okay. Whether we have the thing we believe we need in order to be happy (a partner, money, a certain job, a certain house, a certain level of health, whatever), we begin to cultivate a sense that who we are in this very moment is perfect, complete, and whole.

I think where some of us get stuck is thinking that acknowledging we are okay without the external thing is the final stage. That if we ever want something again, we are focusing on what we don't have. This is an overcompensation for a misunderstanding of dependency and how essential it is to depend on or need others. Because my second point is that, actually, we don't have everything within. And that's also okay. We are not meant to be islands. There are many nights when I have the desire for my beloved to be next to me in bed (and even again this morning). Unless I want to start lying through my teeth, I cannot convince myself that I already have that. I don't. He's not there—I should know. So, to lie there and tell myself "I already have all that I need and want within" is bullshit. I don't. But I *can* feel that desire and still be totally okay with my life. I can be at complete peace while not having what I deeply desire. This is what puts me into a vibrational match for what I want because, rather than focusing on the lack of it, I am actually cultivating my desire for it while knowing I am perfectly okay without it.

So long as we continue to pretend we already possess something or don't actually want it at all, we remain under the impression (even unconsciously) that without it, we are not okay and can't be at peace. We are still "imprisoned," clinging, stuck. We are not free. It's not in desiring that attachment occurs; it's in the grasping of something or pushing it away. It's okay to acknowledge what we don't have and admit what we want. I believe the next stage of enlightenment is to be at complete peace with or without the things we need and want. And this requires that we acknowledge what those things are and allow the feeling of it to permeate us. At times, this might look like feeling into already having something, which so many teachers guide us to do in order to become a vibrational match for it to possibly manifest one day. But let's not forget that doing this sometimes implies we can still only be okay and happy if or when we have the thing we desire.

I sit on my couch, feeling the desire for Michael to come over, be with me, make love to me. I let that desire permeate my entire being while simultaneously noticing how I am still okay with not having it. Equally, I can go beneath these emotions and feel the peace and freedom found in "wanting what I get." Can I want him to *not* be here? Can I be at peace with him not coming? Yes, I can feel that. With tears still wet on my cheeks, I feel a calmness and serenity wash over me as I let myself want (be with) that outcome. After all, I am exhausted from traveling, and the eight-hour jet lag is taking a toll, and going back to sleep sounds delightful. It's not about convincing myself I don't want something (that's still controlling my experience by trying to turn my disappointment into gratitude or indignation); it's about being with whatever is (both my disappointment and simultaneous relief that I get to go back to sleep) and not making it mean something or creating a story out of it.

I hear a voice within me protest, "You can't be okay with him not coming. You need to be angry and sad. He told you he would come, and then he didn't show up. How dare he! This is more proof that you don't get what you want and that it's not safe to want things in the first place!" This voice is very familiar. And I find it quite interesting how this voice isn't okay with me feeling okay. This voice wants me to believe that accepting what is means "bypassing" or ignoring something. That's when I notice how attached some part of me still is to the story that it's not safe to want things because I don't get what I want. This part of me is so attached to "I told you so" that it demands I stay stuck in the feelings associated with it, even if it means giving up my peace.

And then I realize: I'm not actually attached to him coming. I mean, I really wanted him to come. I was excited. I had prepared myself and set the scene. I had imagined the moment for weeks. Yet when he didn't arrive, I was sad, a little angry, and, ultimately, okay. This isn't attachment; it's desire. I wasn't clinging to him coming. I didn't try to force or convince him. I didn't do everything in my power to get him to arrive. Equally, accepting this reality, I don't push him away. I don't shun him out of anger or disappointment. I feel the tears and frustration. I speak into the feelings. I let it be, and then I let it go.

When the masculine is seemingly untrustworthy, what's most interesting is how I now find myself responding. Instead of making it mean something and throwing out everything I have held to be true as I once did, I can hold it lightly. It's not about whether or not I can trust someone; it's about letting whatever is be without exerting myself to find meaning in it, which is a new practice for me. For much of my life, I've made not getting what I want mean something about who I am (like "I'm not worthy"), but if I keep pulling at that string, I usually arrive at "I've done something wrong" or "I'm inherently bad." This is what I'm attached to and imprisoned by. But it can feel scary and insane not to push or pull, to let it be, to let others do what they do in the timing they do it. What would it look like to practice seeing things as just what they are without some grander meaning or explanation? I immediately want to counter that with, "But there *is* a greater meaning to it all." Okay, that may be true ... but what if I allow, as a practice, for things to just be without attaching a meaning or explanation to it? Boy, oh boy, does that feel uncomfy. But I'm willing to give it a shot.

This rewriting of old narratives and reprogramming, reflected back to me by men in my life recently demonstrating their trustworthiness (no matter how long it might take), is starting to feel safer. And yet, I still experience things that seem to directly challenge this new way of being. With Awaken Village Press, I have also been experiencing that sometimes things don't happen in the way or timing I envision (if at all). Enjoying my afternoon gelato and walk around the piazza the next day, I finish up a phone call with my business partner. We are not doing as well as we anticipated we would by this point. For the past month or so, we have been feeling the pressure to bring in more money. If we don't, we could go under in about two months' time. Clint has been in conversations with a potential investor. It would keep us afloat for the rest of the year. Again, I am unable to control the decision this person makes or in what timing. All I can do is hold the vision. Faced again with the challenge of how to hold the faith to create the reality I want, I have another dialogue with my higher wisdom.

"It can feel hard to keep the faith alive sometimes," I admit, discouraged.

"I know. I understand how it will feel, multiple times, like it's the time to give up, throw in the towel," my higher wisdom replies. "But I must remind you, it is by continuing on faithfully that gets you where you end up going."

"I get it. And at times, I can touch that. But other times, I wonder if I'm being … foolish. And, more importantly, I get scared. What if it won't happen?"

"I can feel your hesitation even acknowledging that. You know there's nothing foolish about what you're doing. You're living a life based on faith and trust and receptivity and surrender. There is nothing foolish about any of that. You are always supported. You know this," my higher wisdom reminds me. "The fear is natural because you don't know what's going to happen—you never will. That's part of the game. We watch the game, or even play it, not knowing at all which team will win or who will do what or what the final score will be. That, in fact, is exactly what makes the game worth playing. And, since you are both teams, you will always win."

Wanting what I get, getting what I want—I'm learning doesn't matter. The lesson is to realize I'm okay no matter what, and, because of that, I'm free to experience any and all of it. It is what it is. I might modify Walsh's quote to go something more like this: "Freedom isn't getting what you want; it is wanting what you want, sometimes getting it and sometimes not, and being okay either way." Not quite as succinct, but perhaps more comprehensive.

Two days after that early morning of deep work, Michael unexpectedly knocks on my front door. Unlike before, I'm not ready. I haven't prepared myself or the space. I suppose that's just how it is sometimes. I'm not in control, right? Taking a deep breath, I walk to the door wearing only my bathrobe and glasses. Three years of anticipation overshadows my unpreparedness. I open the door, and our eyes lock. He hasn't changed a bit. Seeing him for the first time in years is like a dream. He steps in, taking my hand, and leads me upstairs, removing my bathrobe before laying me on the bed. He makes love to me for the first time. No candles are lit. No playlist is on. And yet, it's another moment of pure bliss. In that telltale physical experience, I find myself simultaneously shaking with laughter as tears fall onto his chest.

As we lie there together, I can feel how conflicted he is. I know we have both been looking forward to this moment for months—years. I'm still taking in the bliss of this long-awaited moment when he reluctantly tells me he still isn't fully available or ready. He doesn't know how long this might take, and that I should enjoy the possibilities of pleasure that *are* ready for me right now. It isn't what I want to hear, but I honor him and where he's at. I know I don't get to control him or the timeline, as tempting as it is. He's on his own journey, and it has nothing to do with me. Unlike with my other Michael, I know now that it's not up to me to love him enough to free him from his circumstances.

After one last embrace, he leaves. I take his advice to heart. What if I hold what I want dearly and see what happens? What if I allow myself to en*joy* and experience pleasure while "waiting" for more of what I want to arrive? What if living my life, enjoying my life, doing what is best for me means simply being more present? Why deny myself something in the present out of uncertainty about the future? Being more present invites more letting things be. I am once again exploring the Land of Unadulterated Acceptance, this time focused less on accepting myself and more on accepting what is. I can't control when (or if) this man will be ready, but, as before, I won't put my life on hold while I wait.

I have seen how, in so many ways, I want to believe that if I do or say the "right" thing, if I plan or prepare, *then* I'll get what I want, how I want it. Yet Michael has shown me over and over again how this simply isn't true. I don't need to plan or prepare (I mean, I can, and what I plan for might happen, but it might not). Even when I am unprepared, standing at the door in just my bathrobe, I am on the edge of receiving exactly what I have wanted. I can't force things (and even if I do exert control, that's okay—I'm learning I can't fuck things up).

Now, if I still hold the vision, if I see it in my mind's eye, is that control? I don't believe so. That's desire. That's keeping the faith. And what I'm realizing more deeply is that it isn't about whether I "deserve" it. I don't have to "earn" it. I don't have to do things a certain way or not. It'll happen when it happens, how it happens. I am living my life as it is living me. My life is the dancer, and I am the dance.

Thanks to this man, who embodies my desire and clarity, I free myself to live my life and follow my heart, no matter what that means. It might mean traveling across the world. It might mean keeping my heart open and connecting with other men. It might mean letting him go. It might mean speaking my truth. I am continuing to experience that it doesn't matter. I am still having valuable experiences, regardless of what form they take. That's what his presence has offered me: greater clarity that there's an unfolding—even when I can't understand it—no matter what. Obviously, a part of me wants the security in knowing "when," but we rarely get that. And that can't prevent us from living "now."

The months pass as I enjoy another Italian summer and explore the different freedoms available to me, including navigating various types of connections with men, careful not to push too hard any which way. Don't misunderstand me, even when this wisdom flows to and through me, it ain't always easy! Letting things be isn't just "Oh, just let that be, don't worry about it. Que sera, sera!" So, what *does* it mean when I have a desire to do or say something? Does letting my desire be mean doing it, taking action? Or does letting it be mean non-action? See what I mean? It can be a real mind fuck. Do I let be the desire to reach out and resist further action, or do I take action and then let be whatever outcome occurs? Eventually, I realize it's not one or the other. My soft edge is in doing something (or not) and then letting it be. Ultimately the action itself doesn't matter—the thoughts preceding or following do. This becomes my practice: non-choosing—being on the edge of it all.

Now, I *am* still choosing to act or not act, but I no longer remain attached to those choices or the outcomes they may produce. In my current circumstances, this often applies to the choice to send (or not send) a text message. Whichever I choose, can I do so without thinking about it, not holding onto the decision or outcome of that decision? At any given moment, I can make a new choice. Heck, I can decide to send a message after deciding I won't. I can delete a message once I send it (thanks to technological advances). What matters most is how much I suffer over the decision before or after it's made. It doesn't mean I don't feel the sensations that come with the decision or the consequences of my actions; it simply means I don't add additional suffering or torment or anticipation to the process.

I'm rewriting my story that I need to make things mean certain things about who I am. When someone doesn't message me back or seems to pull away, that doesn't necessarily mean they don't like me or that I've done something wrong. It also doesn't mean that I am unlovable or not deserving of what I want. I can release my fear that I'm going to say too much or not enough—I'll probably do both many more times. I can both accept and release my need to be in communication with someone in order to feel more certain about things. I can relax into the knowing that whoever is meant to be in my life will be in my life. I can communicate as I wish to. I will do so no longer from a place of fear but from a place of love. This feels so liberating.

As I feel more stable and secure in these small things, I apply them to other areas of my life. My time in Italy is running out (gotta love tourist visa restrictions), yet I don't currently have a home to return to. I need to leave, but where do I go? When I left Costa Rica to travel back here, I assumed I might return in about three months' time. Interesting. It's the same thought pattern I had back in 2020, except in the opposite direction. I even left a few boxes of belongings with friends in Puerto Viejo to hold onto until I returned, just as I had done here. Yet for some reason, something doesn't feel right about going back. I had thought for sure I was going to return for a friend's birthday party and reunite with my soul family. As I now know so well, October is the best time of year to be on the Caribbean side. But I'm not getting a "yes" in my body. Why am I not getting the green light to book my ticket?

I know by now it's important that I feel internally aligned with my decision and not to force things. I'm learning to listen to my heart, and I know my heart isn't in Costa Rica. But where am I to go if not there? Am I to apply for a digital nomad visa and stay in Europe? Am I to return to the United States? How do I take action or make a decision if there is no "right" choice and it doesn't matter what I choose?

Right "on time," I have a session with my mentor, who wisely and beautifully guides me into a meditative state where I am invited to meet my most future self. Now, since time is an illusion, my "future self" is, in fact, an expression of my "present self" (as that is all there ever is), yet from this expanded state, I am open to channel and receive insight and wisdom that works as a perfect punctuation to this journey I've been on. Sitting on my couch in my quaint top-floor apartment in Vicenza, I approach this most future version of me. She wants to tell me that I don't have to try and figure anything out. She wants me to know there are no questions I need to ask or have answered. She wants me to know there's not some meaning I'm missing or a message I'm not getting. It's a lot simpler than I think. That doesn't mean it's easy, it's just so much simpler. One day, she says, I'll know what that feels like.

She seems so at peace. I ask her, "How are you like this?" She says, "Because I don't have to think about things like that anymore. It's all going to happen exactly as it's meant to happen, and it's going to surprise you, and it's not always going to make sense, and sometimes it will delight you because it makes perfect sense. Sometimes you're going to get exactly what you want, and sometimes you won't. And it's not going to matter because you're here to live it, not to know how it ends."

As I prepare to make my decision—to just do something—I feel a strong pull to fly to Florida and visit my brother, just as I had done when I left Italy in early 2020 before going to Costa Rica. It is beginning to feel like my journey is going in reverse (or perhaps coming full circle). All I know is I want to land somewhere. I want to relax. And I want to do it where the masculine can take care of me. So I book my ticket from VCE to MCO. As I now seem to have a pattern of doing in each town and country in which I live and build community, I gather a few of my closest girlfriends together for a "Ciao for Now" party to celebrate my Vicenza family I've grown to know and love so well.

Within days, the man I once followed to Europe tells me he is also returning to the United States. He got a job on the East Coast and will be moving there in a couple months' time. We had reconnected during the past week after not speaking much, meeting for a coffee and some final Italian shopping (including a lovely pair of sneakers he bought me). Over the last couple of months, we've each been having our own experiences on our respective journeys as I trusted the unfolding of it all. Now, he tells me he will be leaving Italy, and his wife, a month after my own departure.

I am not "choosing" to move back to the U.S. I am also not "not choosing" it. I am not pushing it away or pulling it toward me. I no longer believe the answer is found in choosing exactly what I want and then going for it. Instead, I find that whatever I choose is a part of a happening. And that's when everything that is meant to happen does happen. No matter what it might be.

CHAPTER 16

GIVING UP

My heart is breaking. Again. It's winter, and instead of being depressed in dreary Italy, I'm experiencing the darkness in sunny Florida. After all my yammering about "let it be" and "what happens happens," things are not going the way I had envisioned.

I followed my heart to see the man I love once he arrived in November. After an amazing night together in New York City, we drove to Virginia, where he would be starting his new life as a single man, and I helped him move into his new home. After staying in contact for weeks and nearly visiting him again later that month, I surprised him on Christmas Day by showing up at his place uninvited and unannounced. Apparently, not everyone loves surprises as much as I do!

Once the initial shock wore off, we enjoyed some lovely wine and conversation before we discussed my plans (which I didn't have) and how it would be best for me to leave the following morning. As with other times I haven't gotten what I wanted exactly as I wanted it, I felt my feelings and accepted his need for space, and the universe conspired to get me back to my brother's in an affordable rental car he offered to pay for. Over the past couple of weeks, I have exchanged more dreams and desires with him, including living together and building a life together. He has continued to pull back and put up his walls. He doesn't want the pressure of that right now. He doesn't want to be responsible for the choices I make with him in mind. He doesn't want to keep breaking my heart even though that's what's happening.

I have cried for days and days on end. I feel the depths of loss and sadness that, once again, my visions (which feel so close) aren't being realized in my life. It seems like everything in my life is falling apart or falling away. My business collapsed a few months ago as the necessary investments didn't come through. My team has dissolved. I'm back to just me, a solopreneur with no clear path forward or motivation to continue creating the vision and the village I've held for so long. And now, the man I want to be with is withdrawing again. All the dreams I have been holding for this partnership and what I had imagined would happen once he was no longer with his wife, as well as the growth and expansion of my company, are crumbling all around me. As my mom has wisely told me, things don't always go the way we want or hope. A part of me feels this is a very disenchanted, defeated way of looking at life. Equally, I believe she's right. Life doesn't always—or even often—go as planned.

Returning to the United States is starting to feel more full circle than I originally expected. My brother's home is serving as another cocoon for the final stages of this metamorphosis. A stay that started off as "just a few weeks" as I figured out the next step has quickly expanded to a few months. After traveling a bit to visit some friends and clients, I begin to fear I am experiencing once again what happened to me when I moved in with my parents all those years ago, except this time, I'm without the "security" of a relationship and, instead, feeling the insecurity of what will happen with a new one (or not). Being here at another family home felt initially like a wave of surrender and relaxation, but I know what I truly yearn for is a home of my own. I don't want to repeat the same thing and get stuck here, and with no viable options or resources to provide an alternative, I'm afraid I will. But, as we've all heard, it's darkest before the dawn. I may have returned to the States knowing I'm not in control of how things will unfold, but I have had faith. That slippery, etheric, endlessly frustrating faith.

I find myself sobbing as I watch movies that involve love stories (and most do!). I walk down the street and see elderly couples holding hands, and tears start streaming down my face. I am so tired of feeling the deep heartache of not having what I want. By this point, I know it is okay to want what I want. Still, not having it hurts. I have jumped through all the mental loops to see how I already am what I'm looking for, that I *am* love, and letting the rest be. Still, it hurts. I mean, what more do I have to do (or not do)?

One night after watching a documentary with my brother, I cry so hard it feels as if my chest will literally crack open. This must be why Buddhism talks about freeing oneself of desire. If I didn't have the desire to share my life with this person, create a home with him, have a child with him, I wouldn't feel all this pain, all this heartache when he pulls away, when I must continue to live in the complete uncertainty of it all. Once again, I find myself thinking, "Why even have desires? I should free myself from this desire in order not to feel the pain. If I didn't want a partner and a child, I wouldn't feel sad for not having them."

The next day, the emotions stop. There are no more tears. I feel numb. Instead of feeling things deeply and painfully, I feel nothing at all. Getting through the day (and week) feels hard, like something I don't want to do. I go through the motions, completely disconnected from my purpose or why I'm even here. I feel lost, unmotivated, disenchanted with creating anything. I don't care about Awaken Village. It feels so distant, so far removed from me. I've lost my focus, my desire, my vision for it. It's as though I've held the vision long enough, and I'm over it now.

I once again feel alone in the process. Does anything matter? Nothing seems worth living for. Ultimately, I realize I don't care about anything at all. These thoughts and realizations are very unsettling. It is a very uncomfortable place to be. I don't care what happens or doesn't happen. This is the saddest part of it all. It feels like apathy and depression. Feeling connected to desire, purpose, and meaning is what gets us out of bed in the morning. Life now feels meaningless. With meaning comes a sense of certainty, of control; with no meaning comes a sense of complete surrender. And this form of surrender feels scary at first. It feels very destabilizing. At times, it feels unbearable. I wish I could channel Dido right now, but I can't. I put my white flag above my door. I surrender. I don't want to do this anymore. I give up, which is one of the scariest things to me. And yet, isn't that what surrendering is? Giving up?

It all comes to a head on Friday, the 13th of January. With tear-stained cheeks, I send the same message to both my business partner and the man I love. "I give up. I give up on Awaken Village. I give up on being a mother. I give up on my dreams." This isn't what I want, but I don't know what else to do. How else do I surrender without giving up on my dreams? Clint responds: "Let it be." Lying in bed, wanting to fade away and maybe never wake up, reading these words brings a wave of tears up from deep in my belly. As much as this isn't what I want to hear, it's exactly what I need. It just takes me a moment to realize that.

I continue to think about his response. It isn't, "Let it go." Clint isn't telling me to let go of my vision. He is reminding me that all I can do is let it be; there's nothing I need to do about any of it. He's inviting me to be with all of it—my sadness, my depression, my lack of motivation. This isn't giving up on my hopes and dreams; this is me giving up my self, giving up the fight, putting my hands in the air, waving my white flag because I want to live.

I have thought that waving my white flag of surrender means I am defeated, that I am no longer to have dreams or desires. But it actually means I want to live to see those dreams come to pass; otherwise, I would just keep fighting to the death. It feels like an important place to reach to feel the pain of giving up on all the things I've become attached to on my soul's path, specifically the timing and the way my dreams will manifest. "I don't care" can feel terrifying and liberating at the same time, but it's a natural part of the cycle. Freedom is found when we no longer care what happens. By feeling the scary, vulnerable pain of giving up those attachments, I experience again how I am still alive without them, but I know this isn't where I am meant to stay. The only thing that keeps me going is knowing I've been here before and trusting this must be yet another version of what transformation feels like.

I've done quite a bit of contemplation around the concept of desires—thinking that if I just avoid wanting things (which usually means pretending I don't want something), then I can avoid the pain of not having them or one day losing them. But that's not how it works or what I'm here to experience. And thankfully, I've had much more practice by now. I am able to catch myself in the act. I quickly notice this part of me that wants to dismiss or ignore or throw out my desires in a futile attempt to save myself from feeling pain or discomfort. What *is* is that I have desires, and sometimes (most times) those desires guide me as a lighthouse.

Instead of wanting to free myself from desire, I'm beginning to wonder what's wrong with having it. Wanting to free myself from desire is wanting to free myself from pain, but what's wrong with pain? Many of us are seeking freedom from something, which can often be simplified as "pain." But freedom does not mean freedom from pain. This journey of life is one where pain will continue to arise. What we can experience is freedom from the *fear* of pain.

Ultimately, I'm waving my white flag at myself. This battle has been with me, and I don't want to fight with myself anymore. I fall to my knees and raise my flag, declaring, "I want to live. I want to go on. I just can't go on like *this* anymore." Eventually, I feel a shift from "I don't care what happens," as in hands up, defeated, "nothing matters," to "I don't care what happens," as in "I'm moving forward no matter what." Same words, very different energy.

Through the disintegration of my dreams, I am able to see even more clearly what it is that I *truly* want. For years, I have devoted time and energy to creating a business, having dreams for it to grow into something far beyond me. All my creative energy has flowed into this part of my life. And now, standing amidst the rubble, I look around and ask myself anew: Is this where I want my energy to flow? As much as I love and feel called to do the work I do, serving others in a beautiful way, I hit my deeper truth. At this time in my life, what I want to direct my life force energy into is creating a family. And as a single woman in her forties, this is a very vulnerable place to be.

I'm remaining securely and more confidently attached to my dreams, my visions, my heart's desire, my inner knowing. I don't have to give up on these things. If there's one thing to "hold onto," to "grasp," it is our dreams. These we do not want to let go of. Of course, how we hold them matters. We don't want to crush our dreams or break them by holding on too tightly. Equally, we don't want to drop them or let them go.

I know I often get stuck here because I don't want to let go of someone or a dream or a vision I have. But I start to see that it's not about letting a person or ideal or vision go. It's about letting go of the fighting, the arguing, the belief that I can control another. I'm not here to convince my beloved to love me or see my vision, but I can share it with him. And then I can let it and him be. I'm not here to convince an investor to support Awaken Village or keep my company afloat, but I can share it with them. And then let it and them be. Let the pain be. Let the sadness be. Let the current reality be. Let the dream be. Let the loss be. Let it all be. On the other side of that is where true liberation is found. True letting go, true non-attachment, requires complete acceptance of what is, was, and will be. Letting things be doesn't require any additional effort; it simply requires acceptance and surrender.

I am freeing myself from the heaviness I carry as I surrender to something much larger than myself. I am surrendering to not being in control of my life. I am freeing myself from what has been keeping me from feeling secure in claiming what I want—doubts, lack of trust, overthinking, hesitation, premeditation, fear I would lose myself or something else. I am willing to feel more certain about things while simultaneously letting them be what they are in each and every moment.

I think a part of me secretly hoped that by this point in my story, I would have figured everything out. That it all would make sense. The journey. The heartbreak. The patterns. The experiences. The reason why certain people have come into my life. The reason I have been in other people's lives. The reason I exist. The reason I'm here. I thought this book would give me those answers. I thought I knew how it would end. Me, happily ever after, with everything I ever wanted. Yet that statement alone—"happily ever after"—is so ignorant and untrue. No one can be happy forever.

The point isn't to live a pain-free existence or feel joy in every moment. Michael Singer speaks about pain as the price of freedom in his book *The Untethered Soul*. He considers it a requirement to experience true freedom, not something we are to be freed from. As we open ourselves more and more to where we experience pain, breathing into it, relaxing into it, allowing it to move through us, we are then freed. Again, not free *from* pain, but free *with* pain, which is the greatest freedom of all. I may *not* get everything I ever wanted. That may not be how life—mine included—ends. I don't get to know, and that hurts … a lot. In many ways, it's unacceptable. But, if I can fully accept it, that is also the most freeing thing.

The majority of us live in fear of what might happen if we actually allow ourselves to experience pain. Once we've felt our pain and relaxed into it, letting it move through us, we remember that the pain won't kill us. I'm not saying people don't die from things that also cause pain, but the pain itself doesn't cause the death. Actually, when we resist pain or live in fear of it, we actually tend to perpetuate it, holding onto it and thus feeling it more and more often. This is anxiety. Our fear of it is the thing that keeps it alive. Pain in and of itself, when not hung onto, can often shift and move through us rather quickly. Or, when necessary, we can attend to that pain, and it will eventually stop. It's the suffering, the resistance, that lingers until we choose to no longer be afraid of it.

As much as it hurts sometimes, I *can,* in fact, want whatever I get—whether it's a less-than-ideal reaction to a surprise visit or my company running out of money or the man I love pulling away and cutting off communication. Because no matter what it is, it's information, clarity, direction. I've spent my life looking at how I've done things wrong and created the life I have and the pain I feel. In the past, I would have said, "Amanda, you pushed too hard. You pushed him away," or "You aren't listening. You're not getting the message," or "See?! You know you're supposed to sit back and let it come to you. Now, look at what you've done!" That last one still stings a bit. I am afraid I'm not "learning my lesson," that I am perpetuating my reality. Yet I'm also aware and deeply accepting of the fact that I haven't done anything "wrong"—I've simply done.

Being human can hurt, and that's okay. I'm here to feel everything—that's what it means to be alive. I'm here to experience joy and disappointment, love and loss. Life is going to include pain, heartbreak, loss, and death. We do not become free from this. We free ourselves through this, despite this, thanks to this. We are here to free ourselves from living a sheltered, contrived life where we attempt to avoid this or create an illusion that we can. The purpose of life is not to free ourselves from the desires and disappointments that are inevitable but rather to let ourselves be with all of it, which often means letting ourselves—and "it"—be. If I'm still running around holding onto desires believing that one day they will free me from pain, I'm still trapped. I am freeing myself from the belief that there is some magic bullet that will "save" me or anyone else from this human experience.

By my 41st birthday, I'm beginning to feel a bit better even though my life has not unfolded how I thought it would by now. Once again, I'm without my beloved. Still, it's perfect exactly as it is—a quieter celebration than the last, focused on self-care and a nice dinner with my brother. I witness some small part of me feels confused, though. In some ways, I'm living my ultimate fear—going through the world letting things be, without the stories and beliefs that have shackled me all my life. I don't take what's happening personally. I don't make it mean something about me. I just let it be. Letting it be doesn't mean not having feelings or a response; it simply means not dwelling on it or picking at it.

More than a year has now passed since Michael reentered my life and everything felt like it was coming together. Despite what has happened (and what hasn't), I know this is all happening for me. More than that, it is simply a happening. I don't need to investigate it or unpack it more than that. I can just let it be. I can free myself from believing it means more than it is in this moment, which is a natural sequence of endless vibrational pulses (the yes/no, on/off, something/nothing of life). I mean, everything ebbs and flows constantly, right?

What has happened has happened how it has happened. There is nothing good or bad about it. It doesn't mean anything about me or others in my life. It simply is. It is one in a lifetime of happenings. Everything in nature has its own time, its own cycle and rhythm. In a way, this form of knowing can give way to less control, not more (a huge "aha" for me). Years ago, when releasing my first Michael, I thought "letting go" looked a certain way. Now, I am reminded once more how that isn't something I can force. It is not my job to let this Michael go; it is my responsibility to let him be.

While taking my morning walk through the overhanging trees draped with Spanish moss along the lake near my brother's house, I'm reminded of something else Alan Watts talks about. When we choose to trust nature (including human nature), we trust that, through the chaos, there is order. Now, that doesn't mean storms won't occur or diseases won't spread or animals won't kill each other, but it's all part of the harmony inherent in nature. So, too, this will occur within the human race itself, as we are nature. But if we run around constantly afraid of this happening, afraid that we can't trust ourselves or each other, we miss out on the freedom that exists here and now.

I choose to trust nature (the good and the bad), which means I'll be let down or disappointed. But I would rather go through life like this than not trusting. By the time I return to his house, I return to trusting that all is guided. There is truly nothing to fear; our fear simply points us to where we are still not free. I can't fuck it up; therefore, I can act spontaneously in each and every moment. What I truly desire is to free myself from my incessant thinking and keeping my desires at arms' length. I no longer need the protection they have provided; not because I'm no longer afraid, but because I know I can handle everything. Now, that feels like freedom.

CHAPTER 17

ACTING WITHOUT CHOOSING

"Just because you don't need to figure it out or understand it doesn't mean you won't have epiphanies or 'aha' moments," the voice of my channeled future self expresses through my laptop speakers as I listen back to the recording of my session with my mentor from six months back. "Those are going to continue to occur and delight you, and they will energize you and serve as little yummy treats along the way, but you don't have to seek them out or look for them; they will simply appear and show themselves. Live and experience everything you've learned and understood up until now. That has been the foundation, and it has served you so that now you can move forward boldly."

Much like when I knew the safety of my parents' house was no longer serving me, I know I need to leave this cocoon, which has provided me the external safety and security I needed for the past few months while I deepened my internal feeling of safety and security. More healing has occurred. This time around, I have been able to receive more openly, lean into my femininity more fully, and trust more deeply that my presence alone is enough—that I'm worthy to receive even if I'm not "doing anything." It's time to once again spread my wings and fly, trusting that the wind will carry me. Yet again, I have no idea what to do or where to go or how I will pay for it. I'm still a bit scared and worried, and I know this will never not be true. Each and every time I take a leap of faith, I will feel this flutter of fear and excitement. That's normal and human. And the more often I do it, the more normal it becomes. As I'm learning to do by now, I don't need external confirmation; I simply listen to my heart, act, and trust the universe will conspire to meet me, as it has each time before.

My heart feels drawn to Washington, D.C., but it is a different sensation from years past, driven by feelings of chasing or being dragged. I have visited the city over the past few months during brief periods of contact with Michael, and I immediately liked it. I even found myself thinking, "If I were to move to D.C., I would live in Capitol Hill." I quickly research some options, feeling into each choice and trusting my internal "yes/no." I find a few furnished short-term places, all far more expensive than I feel I can afford. How am I supposed to move forward boldly? I remember this feeling from years back and how the means often have a way of showing up for me when I commit to my desire.

I am clear that if I do choose D.C., it is for me and of my own accord—but why would I move there? It's expensive. I don't know anyone there other than one person who may or may not be available for me to be in his life right now. And he and I are both clear I am not to make this decision based on him. I think about my soul family (and belongings) in Costa Rica, but each time I ask myself if that's where I'm meant to go, I feel a "no." I don't understand it.

I see my fixation on understanding, on how I have lived a life of feeling that in order to have, be, or do anything, I must first make sense of it. It's like if I don't understand how it works, then it's not going to work. I notice how this has been wrapped up in my belief that I must prove myself worthy. If I can prove that I understand, then I've proven myself worthy to receive the ultimate prize—love. If I can figure out the mystery, the puzzle, then I win; I get what I want. But if I don't figure it out or understand it, the opposite will happen—I lose.

As I am trusting my intuition and preparing to take the leap, I continue to be in contact with the man I can't seem to shake. Our dynamic continues to be complicated and fraught with ups and downs, pushes and pulls, ons and offs. As I tend to do, I attempt to make sense of it and share my insights with him, and then lovingly call myself out. "I'm just proving how intelligent I am," I say. "You do not have to prove anything," he tells me. I know he's right, but I can see how desperately I want to show how smart I am, that I "get it." That I understand, so I am worthy of his love. After decades of doing this, I am exhausted.

We spend most of our lives proving who we are. "I'm Amanda. I am a female in a female body who identifies as a female. I am forty-one years old. I run a company. I enjoy traveling and adventure. I am smart. I am a good person. I deserve this. You can trust me." But here's the thing: we only feel we need to prove something when we doubt its "is-ness." In a philosophy course I took in college, we were asked to prove God's existence. It's very difficult, if not impossible. "You just believe," someone said. "Have blind faith," added another. That's not much to hang your hat on, yet it is a very wise statement. It can't be proven, and, ultimately, if you believe it to be true, there is no need to prove it because you have faith that it is. We tend to commit to our beliefs and then go around trying to prove them right. But what if there is nothing to prove?

Faith is rooted in deep knowing and trust without proof. I sought proof of God before I knew there is something larger going on. Then, when first considering how I am a part of all that is, I looked to the universe to prove it to me through synchronicities because I still doubted its "is-ness." Equally, if I don't believe someone loves me, I seek proof of their love for me. If I know they love me, they need not prove anything. If I'm drinking coffee, I'm drinking coffee. If rain is coming from the sky, rain is coming from the sky. If God exists, God exists. If I'm an aspect of the divine, I'm an aspect of the divine. If we're all connected, we're all connected. If I am worthy, I am worthy. If everything is a happening, everything is a happening. What is is; it needs no proof.

Another way we often prove ourselves is by clinging to our past decisions and who we once were. For many of us, we feel "trapped" by our past, meaning we feel stuck in our present circumstances due to our past actions. One could say I am "trapped" by my past decision to "follow" Michael to Italy if it means never following my heart again when things don't go as I envision. Take any decision or action for that matter: buying a house, accepting a job, moving to a new city, declaring your love for someone, showing up unannounced at your beloved's on Christmas. They all have consequences, but if we remain non-judgmental and accepting of what is, we don't have to stay attached to the choice or believe it restricts us from making new choices.

We are never stuck (unless we choose to stay stuck) because we can always do something else. We can stand up and move. We can change our thoughts. We can take a deep breath. We can say something. We can write something. We can cry. We can scream. We can dance. We can cook. We can stop. We can start. We can stay. We can go. They are all actions with consequences that beget new actions that beget new consequences—not in a linear sort of way, but in a limitless possibilities sort of way. Whatever we choose, we are not shackled to it. What often prevents us from believing this is our ego—our shame, our guilt, our fear of what people might think or what might happen.

This perception that time is non-linear or based in cause and effect (meaning what we call the past and future is created in the present moment, as that's all there is) is hard for my mind to comprehend at times. Yet it can be freeing in so many ways. This requires a shift from believing or perceiving that we are being driven by our past, which, as Alan Watts suggests, is much like saying a ship is being driven by its wake. It's a bit of a mind-bender, I get that. But if we can open ourselves to this perspective, we can see that we are not prisoners of our choices. Rather, they inform the present moment in the same way the wake informs the ship's movement—it describes where it has been, not where it is going. The ship is going where the ship is going and may well change course. The indication of where it has been does not dictate its next move any more than the wake of our experience needs to dictate ours. How freeing it can be to realize that past actions do not cause current ones but rather are part of the continuum of life.

If I no longer feel trapped by my previous experiences, I am free in this now moment to choose and do as I please. This is how we free ourselves in each and every moment. Be presented with information.

Make a choice. Release the choice once made. Face the consequences of said choice. Receive more information. Make a new choice. Be with the consequences or outcome of that choice. Receive more information. Make another choice. And on and on we go. The trick is not to get stuck in the "choosing" game, the game that has us believe that we can choose a "better" or "more appropriate" option, and just choose in each and every micro-moment (or, at the very least, shorten the gap between our actions and lessen what Alan Watts calls "mental wobbling" we restrict ourselves with). Acting without choosing is simply an endless stream of micro decisions, one after another after another, where the decision (or choice point) is hardly recognizable. It's not the decision-making we are so accustomed to but rather the instantaneous decision of the moment.

So, I do just that. I release myself from the "wobble" and book a fully furnished place in Capitol Hill, just as I had envisioned, to try it out and see if this is where I'm meant to stay. And, as always, the means appear to cover my expenses "right on time." I send Michael a message letting him know I'll be living across the river for a bit. Within a couple of weeks, I arrive in Washington with my things. Michael even shows up at the airport and helps me with my bags. It's the perfect time of year—when the cherry blossoms are in full bloom. As I so often do, I fall in love with the city on day one. It reminds me of European cities that I have grown so fond of. Even its architecture recalls my time in Italy, which makes sense, having learned while living in Vicenza how inspired it was by Palladio.

I am also reminded of my time in Italy when, a day later, I am once again told he can't do this. It seems our push/pull dynamic is back in full swing, and again, I didn't come here for him and will allow myself to enjoy the pleasures that are available to me in this present moment. So, this is what I do. I give online dating another go and meet a few interesting people, including a handful of new girlfriends. I find my yoga studio and organic market within a few blocks. I continue serving clients (new and old). Just as with nature, my spring has arrived. I am feeling more energized, optimistic, and, with some roots in the ground, ready to see things begin blossoming in my life.

Once we shift our perception that we are part of a happening, a continuum, we can liberate ourselves from believing it is up to us to "choose right" or "choose best." I realize that acting without choosing feels a lot like having faith. When we have faith, we act without over-thinking, trusting that the step will appear. We act without controlling the outcome, having faith that we will be able to handle whatever happens. We act with a knowing that whatever happens next "is what it is." We act without gripping too tightly, without needing to justify, defend, or prove our actions. No matter what happens, we are not attached to being right or wrong, good or bad. Just like the Chinese farmer, maybe it goes the way we want and maybe it doesn't. In this way, we just do. And the "choice" is practically instantaneous.

So, non-choosing is both different from "not choosing"—as in avoiding making a choice for fear of what might happen if we do—and simultaneously similar. It's similar in that most of us don't sit here contemplating, "Should I inhale now or not?" or "Should I beat my heart now or not?" It seems to get more complicated when we believe an action is no longer an involuntary one, that we are separate from it.

As I learned from one of my first clients back in 2018, there are four levels of consciousness: life is happening to me, life is happening by me, life is happening through me, and life is happening as me. I've come to see how this is less of a pyramid or quadrant and more like a circle where the first level and last level (or box) are actually one and the same. In a way, when we get to "life is happening as me," we see how "life is happening to me," not from a sense of victimhood but rather from lack of separation between that which happens involuntarily and that which happens voluntarily. What is happening *to* me is happening *as* me. "As me" points to how we are both the doer and the doing or the creator and the creation. It is happening *to* us as the creation, the doing, and it is also happening *as* us as the creator, the doer. Just like how our gut is happening "to us" (meaning we aren't controlling it or even stopping to see if it is a "good" thing that is happening), our gut and digestion are also happening "as us." It's not much different than if I "voluntarily" wander aimlessly around my neighborhood or move my arm around—I'm simply acting without stopping and choosing which way to go or move my body next.

I've had many opportunities over the past few years (and even few weeks) to make a choice most of us would likely deem "big"—where to live, when to travel, who to spend time with, who to commit my heart to. And now I'm faced with yet another one. It's been over four years since I signed a lease on an apartment and claimed a place as a "permanent home." My two months are coming to an end, and I need to choose what to do next—without getting stuck in the choosing.

After visiting a few apartments per a new friend's recommendation, I come across the perfect one. It has everything I want and more—even an infinity pool. Still, I'm scared to pull the trigger and sign a lease. But I figure I just need to do one thing at a time—ask my brother if he'll co-sign, receive information, do the next thing, fill out the application, receive more information, release the outcome. Filling out the application brings up emotion and fear to the point that I have to stop and take a break. I realize the idea of committing to a place like this—not knowing where the money needed to sustain myself will come from month after month and also acknowledging that my life doesn't fit neatly into a standardized application—is a very emotional thing for me. I decide to give myself a few hours, far less time than I have spent on decisions in the past, to let my nervous system relax. Then, I submit the application with my brother as a co-signer. I will let the universe determine the rest. Less than twenty-four hours later, I receive confirmation that my application has been accepted. My entire body lights up, which gives me a lot of information. I have a new home for the next fourteen months, and I am still unsure if I will have someone to share it with.

Sometimes action happens faster or slower, with less or more "wobbling of the mind." At the end of the day, I do take action. And this time, I notice a difference. The less I hesitate, the less anxiety I feel. Ultimately, even when we fool ourselves into thinking we've weighed all our options before choosing to do something (which is impossible because there is an infinite amount of them), the actual decision happens instantaneously. We may deliberate and engage in mental gymnastics for hours, days, even years. But the actual decision—to buy the house, to book the flight, to accept the job offer, to declare one's love—is made at that exact moment. It's an instantaneous decision. In this way, whatever we do from this state of being isn't so much a choice as it is a spontaneous action, which is our key to liberation. And it is up to us how much trepidation there is before we unlock our shackles.

I have, at times, assumed that acting without choosing would mean acting without desire—aimlessly drifting along with no vision or north star. But I've learned this isn't the case. The primary way we imprison ourselves is by denying our heart's desires by doing something else. It is up to us to feel these desires or not, express them or not, and follow them or not. Isn't it the fear of "but if I just do whatever I want to do, I'll do something wrong" the very thing that keeps us believing we aren't sovereign? If we just act, we might get hurt or hurt others. Here's the thing. We will get hurt. We will hurt others. There's no way to avoid that. No amount of mental wobbling will prevent pain or loss (ultimately), and isn't that what so many of us are believing is true? "If I choose this, then I'll be better off." Instead, what if we simply align action with desire in each and every moment? In this moment, I desire to land and have a home. So, I sign a lease. In this moment, I desire to have dinner with someone, so I send a message. See how that works?

I can imagine some might worry that if we all live this way, people will run around being jerks and hurting people. Well, first of all, I'm sorry to say, that is already happening. Secondly, I'm not advocating people act out or cause harm simply because they are "doing as they please." My prayer is that each of us continues to do the work required to take radical responsibility for our feelings, triggers, reactions, and actions. But the truth is, most of us overcompensate a bit in this regard, especially if we've been doing work on ourselves, and that's when we get stuck when faced with taking action or giving ourselves permission to be who we are.

Over the next few weeks, I am in communication with my dear friend in North Carolina whose eye for design I love. She knows how to create beautiful spaces, and each time I've been in her home, I have felt so held and comfortable and nourished. When we first met many years ago, she told me she would help me decorate and create my space—and now the time has come. With my input, she picks out all the things my new home will need for me to feel the way I feel when I visit hers.

Michael's still not ready, but we update each other on our lives from time to time, and I express gratitude for how he continues to be a mirror for me (yet another guru in my life). I share that I have decided to stay nearby for at least the next year and ask if he would help me move, since I desire the strength of a man to support this effort. He replies, "I'll help." I arrange things for the move, including the things I need to buy as well as the rental van I load up. Within forty-eight hours, and thanks to these two individuals I couldn't have done it without, the entire place is unpacked, decorated, and ready for me to call home.

Freeing myself means my thoughts and actions are in service to my heart's desires and to the inspiration I receive. It means allowing myself to savor the sensation of that love and desire, which sometimes also hurts like hell. As I continue to share my feelings with Michael, he once again communicates he can't give me a timeframe and doesn't want to keep me waiting. I appreciate his concern and honor his inability to predict the future, but he does not view waiting the way I do. I also appreciate that I can share what I share and want what I want and do what I do, even if he can't meet me or give me that.

For many years, I unconsciously (and then consciously) believed I could free men by loving them unconditionally. I figured that was one of the reasons I kept attracting them when they were unavailable. Thing is, we can't free others if they don't want to be freed. We can unlock the door and even open it, but if they are more comfortable in their cell and prefer to stay put, there's nothing else we can do. What I have eventually come to realize is that by loving others, I'm not freeing them, I'm freeing myself. It's not that I am here to love them free; I simply hadn't yet seen that I desired to love myself free. And part of how I do that is by allowing myself to love and express that love in all its forms, starting with myself.

Freedom is connected to both non-resistance and non-attachment. In a sense, they are one and the same. If I'm resisting something, I'm attached, I'm stuck. From this point forward, I free myself and others to love how we love, feel what we feel, say what we say, do what we do. There is no holding back, there is no protecting ourselves from something, there is no holding on too tightly that prevents us from allowing true love to freely flow. This is non-attachment. This is freedom. Freedom to exist. Freedom to be. Freedom to experience *all of it*.

Unlike what I used to think, it's not the availability of choice that frees us. Too often, we get stuck in the belief that choice implies there is a "right" or "wrong" or a "this" or "that"—something we are "supposed" to do. When I live fully in the both/and, that's as close to truth as I'll ever come—and we've all heard the phrase, "The truth shall set you free." Good and bad, right and wrong, this and that—these all exist simultaneously. No matter what I choose to do, I will still experience the "somethingness" and the "nothingness," the pain and pleasure, the ups and downs, the yes and no of life.

So, if choice is not freedom, what is? Freedom is breaking out of the illusion that there is anything to choose in the first place. Freedom is feeling the sense of relief that whichever way we go will take us exactly where we are going. Freedom is found in embracing all of it rather than believing we can choose our way out of half of it. There is no growth or evolution or expansion without the opposite. That's part of this whole thing. That's what it means to be human.

This journey to becoming free has been multi-layered and cyclical. In some ways, I feel like I'm right back where I started. I used to believe I was not choosing because, inevitably, things would change, including my feelings and desires. This scared me and left me wary of trusting myself. It also kept me from seeing how safe it is to act without choosing, even if that means I'm "wrong." I have since learned to accept the unacceptable truth that the only constant is change. I no longer resist listening to and following my desires and instead embrace them as part of life.

Everything will change, including myself. I know this. Still, I act and respond to life. I move through it without needing to understand, knowing what I do next simply requires acting without choosing. Even through all of my own changes, I see the constants that have always been—I have made decisions, faced the consequences, changed my mind, and taken new actions. In a way, I realize I have been free this whole time, and the only thing that has changed is my perception of it all. I am free to choose whatever I want, but choosing is different now. Now, I'm choosing myself in each and every moment. I'm choosing to listen to and trust myself and my heart's desires as an extension of nature and all that is. And in this moment, that nature is reflected all around me in the cherry blossom trees of the beautiful city I have chosen to call home.

CHAPTER 18

UNSHACKLED

Living again in this "ordinary world," my home country where this journey began all those years ago, it's clear things will never be as they once were. I have returned with the treasures I have revealed along the way—now, more than a few boxes' and suitcases' worth. My new home is filled with beautiful things, just as I've imagined and desired for many years. It just took some time for me to accept that it is safe for home to be more than just where I am. I am no longer afraid to hold onto something, someone, or someplace. Equally, I am not afraid to follow my heart and to love fully and deeply each step of the way.

Often, when we think of a journey (or even life), we envision the hero setting off and never coming back. We see the person heading out into the sunset, never to return again. What's fascinating to me is that the hero's journey, which is such a beautiful way to "make sense" of our life experiences, is a circle, not a line on a graph. This is why life often feels like we're going around in circles because, in a way, we are. It isn't about getting somewhere—it's about getting to know oneself more deeply.

Setting out on the journey to becoming free wasn't intended to end with me being an entirely different person with an entirely different life. This is the life I have even though it now contains more belongings. The intention is to come back to where I started, to the life I've "chosen," with a completely new perspective, understanding, and tools.

When I began this journey, I thought becoming free meant divorcing my husband, moving from place to place to place, owning very few possessions, hiking the entire Appalachian Trail with my boyfriend, traveling for work each and every week, taking vacations and seeing beautiful places all around the world, and eventually quitting my corporate job with no Plan B. Essentially, not having anything "holding me back"—a person, a job, stuff. I believed external things (and even internal desires) inhibited my freedom to choose whatever I wanted at any given moment.

I thought freedom meant stripping myself of external security in order to find security within (which *is* an important part of the journey, but I've learned it's not the end). I thought freedom was found in the nothingness, in lack, in deprivation. I didn't believe I could be free *and* have specific desires or things. But I've realized that if I am lying to myself, I am not free. And I've been lying to myself for a long time. I've lied to myself by convincing myself I don't want or need certain things in life (like soft furry throws or multiple plants or a partner) as well as believing stories and beliefs that aren't true. Now that I have greater security within, I can have and want these external things without feeling held back or trapped by them. True freedom is found as I unshackle myself from these lies.

One of the stories I've believed is that it isn't safe to express myself, that I will push people away or smother them. The truth is, sometimes I will and sometimes I won't. And I have come to realize that one of the things I value most is having the freedom to express myself—saying what I want to say, creating what I want to create, going where I want to go, loving who and how I want to love—which is a freedom only I can grant myself. It's already here; it's simply whether or not I see it or honor it or choose it. This is probably the reason why "being good with being me" became my tagline back in 2015 when I first stepped out on my own as an entrepreneur. It became my motto, my practice, my "abhyasa." It's taken me years to more fully integrate and embody this mantra, and it will continue to be my lifelong practice, I'm sure.

As I release myself from the false beliefs and stories that have kept me from expressing myself freely, I am able to listen to and follow my soul's desires. While we aren't here to hang our happiness on getting everything we want, we are here to be honest with ourselves about what we want and express it more fully to ourselves and others. As I keep learning, it's not about getting what I want (as in everything going my way), it's about wanting what I get (the full spectrum of being human). Even with my relationship from almost five years ago, I didn't always realize it at the time, but I wanted what I got—for that relationship to grow and expand me. But being at peace with and not fighting what is doesn't mean I can't want something. This is the paradox. Once we feel secure in ourselves and accept that we are ultimately okay no matter what, we are free to admit and express our needs.

While settling into my new apartment, full of so much beauty, I feel an emptiness. After more than a decade of feeling free to do as I please whenever I please, I have started to notice that I have been avoiding something. My understanding of freedom has been holding me back from acknowledging something deeper. Even though I have felt free to do whatever I please, still something is missing.

I am reminded of something my future self had shared with me. Regarding my current needs and whether they're being met, she said, "Oh, honey. You have certain things you need, many of which you have. Your need to be doing work in the world that matters and contribute your gifts is being met magnificently. You feel so seen by friends and others you interact with daily. You are getting so much novelty and adventure. But I can see and feel how desperately you need to feel stable and supported very tangibly by another person in your life. In the mundane things. I see your need for physical partnership, intimacy, and connection. I know you need to be physically supported, whether that's being held in someone's arms or being given physical things or being provided with money or food or hugs or kisses. I know that's missing from your life right now in the way that you want. You need to feel that partnership, to know that you're not going through life alone, that you have someone to make decisions with, share your day with, bring things into creation with. I know you need that, and you don't have it yet."

Her words brought me to tears. This need has been a huge part of my journey—the "missing piece." I now know and feel how safe it is to want this, to need this, to express this. I am at peace with both what is *and* with needing this in my life. I am freeing myself from the shackles of shame I've worn for so long. Shame that I need a partner. Shame that I desire a child to pour my love into and be fully present with and for. Shame that I desire to be provided for by others so I may nurture others and express my gifts even more fully so that I can be a partner and a mother and a book doula and whatever other forms and expressions of love I am called to. It is interdependence at its finest. I am here to love. I am here to be loved. I am here to give life. I am here to receive life. This is what it means to be human—to be a part of the larger whole.

And the only way I can receive what I want is by releasing myself from the belief that it isn't okay to want this, that in some way it's not okay for me to receive from others, to be taken care of, to have a child, to not just do it myself. Oh, how deep this conditioning and programming runs. In order to have what I want, I must make it happen, whether that refers to making money or creating my home, believing it's entirely up to me whether it all comes to fruition. But what if that weren't true anymore? There are so many ways nature expresses itself, and each part of nature plays its part fully without shame or fear. Humans are no different, each playing their role, as did my brother serving as my financial lifeline, my best friend contributing her time and gifts to create my fabulous space, Michael and other men serving as my gurus so I can more clearly see myself.

I am a visionary. I am a dreamkeeper. I create through faith. And with this comes clear vision and possibility of what could be, knowing deep down what's possible. I believe in my visions and dreams. This is one of my superpowers, one of the unique gifts I have to offer the world. This is what I've been practicing for my entire life and why I'm so tenacious. I can believe it and see it before others can, which is why I'm willing to keep it alive.

Dreamkeepers need materializers and actualizers. I need people in my life who are willing and able to materialize the dream I am holding. Sometimes it can seem like I'm holding it on my own, but that's only because I'm not always able to see how others are playing their own vital roles in bringing this dream to life, in making it manifest. And the materialization of something can take the longest amount of time (whereas having a vision can happen in an instant). This is why being patient is a prerequisite (and, equally, an infuriating challenge) to being a dreamkeeper.

I keep dreams alive not only for myself but for others, including my clients, business collaborators, friends, and lovers. So long as they play their role to actualize it or build it or materialize it, I'll keep holding the dream, protecting it for them as they face the frustrations and discouragements of their own journeys. My role as a book doula is to ask my clients to claim something that might be uncomfortable to claim, to prioritize something they haven't prioritized before. It is time for *me* to fully commit to my dream, even if it's uncomfortable to do so, to prioritize it in a way I haven't before. What I can't do is control it. I am not in control of if or how that vision comes into being, just as my clients or business collaborators or friends or lovers aren't. I can't control if someone chooses me or not, if someone opens their heart or not, if someone lets down their guard or not, if someone stops drinking or not, if someone hires me or not, if someone gives my company money or not, or if I get what I want. ("If" is the key word here and the most uncomfortable part.) But that no longer needs to keep me or others in my life from claiming what we want.

Sometimes life doesn't go as planned. We are not in control of it. I think back to the cocoon of my brother's house, to the games we so often played. How do I play the game of life if I don't understand it? Well, here's the thing—I can understand the "rules" without knowing how it's going to go or why. That's not what playing a game is all about; we don't play if we know the end. All we need is to know the rules and our role. From there, we surrender (sometimes more or less graciously) to how the game unfolds, no matter if it makes sense, and definitely without knowing what comes next. The game isn't about planning every move and then watching it unfold exactly as we thought it would. The game isn't even about understanding what has happened so far or how to prevent it from happening again. I mean, yes, we can learn the rules of chess in order to attempt to protect our king. We can learn strategy in order to win more often. But the game will still surprise us (especially if we're playing with another skilled or passionate player). The game might upset us. Our strategy may not work. Sometimes it may feel like we've lost. But this is why we play games in the first place—for the thrill of the unpredictable.

So, what can I control? What action am I responsible for? Playing full-out. Sharing my dreams, my visions, my truth, and my heart openly with others. If others choose to do something with that information, or if it opens their hearts in a new way, then the vision might be realized as it has with my apartment. It is my responsibility to tell people what I see, how I feel. Speak from my heart as often as possible. And then let it be.

What I have read and heard about for years now, I am finally experiencing. I now know what it feels like to love something more "truly" when I am securely attached to it. I am free to be more of who I am, which is love. To love more deeply and fully. And what deeper or fuller way can love be expressed than through that of a child? By two becoming one.

For a few days, I feel sad and lonely, not knowing why the game is unfolding this way, why I now have this home without other key components—a partner and child. Then, as I continue being open to meaningful moments with the people all around me, I accept what is and embrace my new life and the community it does provide, knowing this is a worthwhile fragment of what I am waiting for. As I more deeply surrender, I reveal more of who I truly am, which is one with all that is. When I'm deeply connected to that part of me that knows and trusts that, then I have no reason or need to "figure it out." I simply know. What if this is the place from which to reside? There is no intellectualizing or analysis required. Oh, what a fun circle the paradox of life is! The moment I truly know something, I no longer need to find the meaning or figure it out because I already know it.

So, what do I already know? I am love. I am loved. All is happening as me. I am fully supported and completely safe. I am part of a happening that is unfolding exactly as it's meant to. There is no right versus wrong, good versus bad—there just is. I am both the creator and the creation. My ego and personality have needs and wants and desires and neuroses. I am worthy of all that I desire, and there is no need to cling to or push away these desires. I no longer need to defend or prove my truth. My truth is that I am ready and deserving of partnership and motherhood and having a home. I am ready and deserving of being in my feminine energy. I will experience more fully what it feels like to generate abundance and provision simply for being me (and not just for me but for all those I share my presence with).

My mantra for this year is "Expression of Being," which represents my desire to express my true essence, thoughts, and feelings in my moment-to-moment living. All we have is now. Suffering ends and freedom begins once I accept what *is* instead of getting stuck trying to predict what is yet to come. True liberation is found in "nirvana," the deep exhale when we remember this existence is insoluble.

Ironically, I think I'm beginning to understand now: the search for understanding is no longer necessary once I surrender to my knowing, which is what I ultimately wanted to begin with. I recall the conversation I had with my future self while sitting on my couch in Vicenza, still unaware I would be returning to the United States. She knows and understands how frustrating it feels for me to let go of the need to understand. I asked her how many years it takes me to arrive at her state of peace and surrender and acceptance. "You won't know that, either," she explained. "You don't need to know how long it's going to take or if it's going to happen at all." I paused, sitting on that couch, imagining how it would feel to live life no longer needing to understand things.

Now, many months later, I am ready to add to those words she shared with me. When I am free, life will feel like a dance, a flow. I will be like a martial artist, responding in every moment to whatever impulse or input or stimulus I receive. Whatever presents itself, I will respond without thinking about it. It will just happen. There will be so much less friction and apprehension. I'll stop trying so hard. I won't feel like fighting with myself or anything around me. I'll just relax. My mind will not be spent thinking about moments ago or moments to come. It will be so fully present every single moment to feel what I feel, know what I know, say what I want to say, do what I want to do, and have no need to know what comes next. It will feel like living. I won't fear feeling it all. I will feel joy and sadness and frustration and delight and anger and passion.

As I listen to my wisdom, lounging on my rooftop by the infinity pool, I close my eyes and let myself feel what it is like when I am in that state. I know it impacts my life and the lives around me greatly. I don't get in my own way so much, so I get to experience more of what I'm here to experience. I am honest and present with every single person. I have greater clarity in each moment with that person. I share myself with that person more fully. That person has more information and input to respond to. Like gravity, it brings them into the present moment more fully. The more present I am with others, the more present they get to be with me and others and themselves. And the more present they are with themselves, the more they, too, get to see how magically life unfolds. They witness what it can look or feel like not to need to understand, seeing me being free from that, in the "is-ness" of life.

Any moment we are in resistance (or craving or clinging), we are trapped (just like those darn Chinese finger traps). Any moment we give into previously held patterns, stories, or beliefs, we stay stuck. And maybe all of it—even the beliefs that I'll get what I want by letting go, that I'll never get what I want, that I create my life and am at its mercy, that I am in control and also not—is also just a happening. "It is what it is." There is no pushing or pulling. There is no thinking it ought to be different. There is no resistance.

I take a deep breath in, ready to embark on my next adventure. I still don't know how the story will end (I now realize that's sort of the whole point), but I now know it is part of a continuum. However it looks, I know I will experience greater oneness, greater unity within myself and with another. I don't yet have a relationship with the person with whom I will become one, but if I've learned anything, I do not have to see it in order to believe it. It has already been calling me for many years, but I wasn't ready to heed the call until I freed myself to feel and experience all that life has to offer—the joy and sorrow, the bliss and grief, the other and me. I know that freedom and sovereignty are essential for true union. And true freedom is found when I am free to be me and you are free to be you.

Enjoying the sun on my face, I get in the pool that overlooks the Capitol and smile. With delight, I remember how the dome symbolizes steadfastness and confidence, as well as national unity—all things I'm calling in. Now, I am even more free. I am free to feel secure in my knowing, in my truth, and release the rest. I am free from forcing or letting go completely. I am free to be a dreamkeeper, keeping the vision alive without pushing too hard or throwing it away. I am free to be on the edge of it all—stability and chaos, faith and uncertainty, security and freedom. I am afloat in the sea of possibility. What I choose to do is between me and my creator and is an expression of my sovereignty, not because of or for anyone else. Because nothing is wrong, I am not wrong. And it's never wrong to follow my heart's guidance, to take a step, to move in the direction I feel compelled to move.

"Lead, and I will follow." This is how I continue to live my life. The one leading is my heart, and, at times, it might be represented by someone external. Yet "following," as one does with a confident leader, has a very different energy from "chasing." I'm not actually sure I was ever chasing, but, like many others, I was probably programmed to believe that if I "go for what I want," I'm "chasing it" as opposed to letting it move me. The movement toward something might look exactly the same on the outside, but I now clearly see the difference.

Following my courageous heart, I landed in the heart of America. I could have never guessed I would one day live in our nation's capital. But that's the great thing about not needing to know. Returning from the pool, I stand in the doorway of my studio apartment built in 2020, far from empty. It is the first home I have bothered to furnish and decorate according to my taste and desires. The commitment that brought up so much anxiety in me has also given me the opportunity to create a home that offers me a comfortable place to relax, to just be.

These 450 square feet will serve as my home base for the unforeseeable future. I may have moved into this bright space for myself, but I didn't do it alone. Just as my sun in Pisces in the fifth house would have it, I have held the vision, and so many dear people have supported and provided for me in bringing it into reality. Thanks to the interdependence of things, I feel more grounded in who I am (just as my higher wisdom noted all those years ago). I have grown roots.

While the future is unknown, I have found comfort amidst the discomfort. I free myself to securely know what my heart knows and trust it is on its way to me. With gratitude and a deep exhale, I step inside and close the door behind me, feeling simultaneously confident and uncertain about my future and what lies ahead. My heart, wide open.

ACKNOWLEDGEMENTS

I live the books I write and write the life I live. Because of this, many people went into the writing of this book. For each and every person whose life has served as a source of inspiration, motivation, or connection—thank you. I would not be the person I am today, nor would this book exist, if it weren't for you.

A special thank-you to those who played key roles in the inspiration and insights for the book. This includes, but is not limited to, my parents, who have loved and supported me through it all; my previous partners, who are mentioned in the book and who have served as teachers and mirrors for me; my brother, for his generous support throughout this journey; my dear friends, who consistently remind me of what is true and help me navigate the ups and downs of life; my soul families in Costa Rica and Italy (and wherever else you may be these days); my mentor and business partner for his insight and support; the men I have loved along the way, inspiring me to clarify who I am and express myself more fully, helping me free myself through loving another.

In addition to those whom I know personally, I want to thank a few of those who have influenced me along the way from afar. Ram Dass, Eckhart Tolle, Michael Singer, Thich Nhat Hahn, the channels of *A Course in Miracles*, and Alan Watts.

Also, a special thanks to those who went into the creation and development of this book. To my editor and book doula, Grace Watson. This book would not be what it is without your loving encouragement, well-trained eye, and skillful approach to the written word. To my mother and proofreader extraordinaire, Marianne Johnson. Thank you for ensuring my books are as perfect as they possibly can be. I am eternally grateful for your contribution to my life's work in so many ways. To my cover designer and illustrator, Andrea Gibb. Thank you for your tremendous gift as an artist and designer, presenting this book in such a beautiful way. Your creative and generous spirit is a blessing. And to Elizabeth Gudrais for offering invaluable feedback during the early stages of this book and then lovingly, joyously, and meticulously supporting the book's layout. I am so grateful for our ongoing collaboration.

ABOUT THE AUTHOR

Amanda Johnson founded Awaken Village Press—an indie publishing house that is here to awaken the planet, one book at a time—after many years serving as a guide, hosting a podcast, and publishing her first book, *Becoming Enough: A Heroine's Journey to the Already Perfect Self.* She continues to hold the vision and serve as a source of inspiration for the village at large and each of the members who have a message or gift to share with the world. In addition to attracting villagers into our ever-growing community, she works one-on-one with authors to bring their unique stories and perspectives into the world in an authentic and compassionate way.

As an author herself, Amanda understands the transformative process of writing and sharing our stories and not just focusing on the final outcome. She believes that when we reveal and express more of who we truly are, we change our world. In her role as a book doula, Amanda is the guide for a metamorphic journey that results in aha moments, clarity of thought, and many lives changed through the process of co-creating a book together.

She has spent the past many years as a digital nomad living in various cities around the globe and is excited to be rooting down at this point in her life. To learn more or get in touch, visit amandajohnson.tv or awakenvillagepress.com.

www.ingramcontent.com/pod-product-compliance
Lightning Source LLC
Chambersburg PA
CBHW031458120626
46545CB00005B/1661